The Best Friend's Guide to
Maternity Leave

OTHER BOOKS BY BETTY HOLCOMB

Not Guilty: The Good News for Working Mothers

The Best Friend's Guide to
Maternity Leave

Making the Most of Your Precious Time at Home

BETTY HOLCOMB

PERSEUS PUBLISHING

Cambridge, Massachusetts

Cataloging-in-Publication Data is available from
the Library of Congress
ISBN 0–7382-0279-7

Perseus Publishing is a member of the Perseus Books Group.
Find us on the World Wide Web at
http://www.perseuspublishing.com
Perseus Publishing books are available at special discounts for bulk
purchases in the U.S. by corporations, institutions, and other organi-
zations. For more information, please contact the Special Markets
Department at the Perseus Books Group, 11 Cambridge Center,
Cambridge, MA 02142, or call (617)252-5298.

Text design by Cynthia Young
Set in 10.5-point Minion by Perseus Publishing Services

First printing, August 2001

1 2 3 4 5 6 7 8 9 10—03 02 01

Dedicated to
Daniel and Rachel
For making my life more wonderful

Contents

Acknowledgments

Many thanks to my editor, Marnie Cochran, for her patience, support, and encouragement—and for coming up with the idea for this book. And many thanks to Flip Brophy, the best agent in the world, who brought Marnie and me together. Without both these wonderful women, this book would never have been born.

Introduction

"When is the baby due?" the cashier at my local bodega inquired, with one of those big, engaging smiles people get when they see you're pregnant.

When is the baby due?

I'd been asked that question so many times in recent months that my response was usually automatic. But not this time. As I stared down at my oversized abdomen and the maternity pants I'd worn for months, I took a deep breath. What could I say? I'd delivered Rachel five days before.

This smiling cashier provided me with a new and more accurate body image, a snapshot of how I appeared to other people in the days after my first child was born. Nine months pregnant, that's how I looked. I was too embarrassed to tell her the truth, and pretty certain that she'd be horrified if I did. So I took the easy way out.

"Any minute now! And I'm so-o-o ready!" I replied in as cheery a tone as I could muster.

In the years since then, I've learned I was hardly alone in this experience. "Ha! Five days! I had it happen to me *four months* after I had Nicky!" my sister-in-law, Chris, told me after I confessed my humiliation. "Can you imagine?" In her case, the question had come from one of her graduate students. The young woman, who had apparently never had kids, hadn't even registered that Chris could not possibly carry a baby for 13 months. Another friend of mine had the big question put to her three weeks after giving birth, as she walked through her company's parking lot.

Still, no one warned any of us we'd still look pregnant after delivery. No one told us we'd still be in our maternity clothes at least a few weeks after the baby arrived, even though this is fairly routine.

Not that these were facts I would exactly have welcomed prior to Rachel's birth. I suppose my more experienced friends were just trying to protect me. They figured some things are better left unsaid. And who knows? Maybe they thought I'd be one of those lucky women who only gained twenty pounds or so and lost it all within a week of the birth.

I do know those women exist. I even knew a few firsthand who were pregnant the same time I was, and returned to work quickly, looking like they'd never had a baby.

But again, my experience is the more common one. I had fifteen or twenty pounds that stayed with me for about a year after both kids. My shape today is very much closer to what it was before I had my children. (Well, I'm not confessing how old I am, and everything about how my body has changed!) I do have a few scars, one from the cesarean the first time around. And, those spider veins. I was spared the stretch marks.

That's it on the body stuff, I promise. No more revelations.

The truth is that none of this bothers me, even though I know it's supposed to, according to the fashion police. Brad Pitt is probably not interested in me. But I love my kids and if a few spider veins came as part of the package, so what?

Still, it would have been useful to know a few more things than I did as I tried to plan my maternity leave. Like the fact that I would still need those clothes with oversized elastic waists for a while longer. I had gleefully passed the best ones along to a pregnant friend, hoping never to lay eyes on them again.

Ever.

I was embarrassed when I had to ask to borrow them back again. They were the only reasonably professional-looking clothes I had that still fit two months after I had Rachel, when I had to go on interviews for an article.

But hanging on to maternity clothes is only one of the tips I wished someone had shared with me. In the pages that follow, I'll share many others, and I promise that nearly all of them will be more important than wardrobe planning. Like how to get enough time and money together so you can truly enjoy your first months with your new baby. That's what this book is all about. Enjoying your new baby. And I hope it will help you do just that.

Chapter 1

How Much Time Will You Need?

When I got home from the hospital, I felt lucky when Daniel went more than two hours without nursing. To survive, I just cradled him next to me and we slept. On the bed, on a couch, in a chair. It didn't matter where. I could have slept on a an ice-cold concrete floor. Like a baby.

That was the first month.

The second month, we woke up.

That's it, my total memory of my first month with my son. Surely, I must have done other things. Answered the phone. Played with, talked to, and fed my six-year-old daughter. Visited with my in-laws, who lived nearby. But my memory of those activities is now based purely on second-hand reports. All I recall is the sleeping part. Oh, and the episiotomy. Lying down was infinitely better than sitting, that I remember. It was another good reason to sleep.

Even when I was awake, I couldn't hold a thought, much less an intelligent conversation. As a writer, I briefly considered publishing a new book. It would be called *Mommy-Think*. All the pages would be blank.

I tell you this, just to clarify one point: If I'd had to get back to work at six to eight weeks, the standard maternity leave at so many companies, I'd have been a wreck. I could easily slump, sleep, sigh, space out, stare at the miracle of this new boy. Those activities suited me just fine. But work? I couldn't imagine it yet. Dan was nowhere close to getting onto a regular schedule. Heck, he wasn't even sleeping through the night at eight weeks, and so, of course, neither was I. My raccoon eyes bore testimony to that—and I have the pictures to prove it. (I don't display them much. I just show the ones of Dan, alone, sleeping.)

Besides all that, he was my second child, and I knew he was my last. I wasn't ready to leave him so soon. It would have broken my heart to go back to work a few weeks after his birth.

So I returned to work gradually, starting with three days a week when he was four months old—with two of those days at home. (Yes, I had a caregiver to help me. No, you can't work with a baby on your lap.) Over the next eight months, I built up to a four-day week. And that's where I stayed for the next few years. A four-day week, with a day or two at home each week.

For me, it was the perfect maternity leave.

What's Best for You?

I'd recommend that arrangement to every new mom, except for two things.

Number one, I know I was darn lucky to get two of my four months of maternity leave at full pay, and to have a husband earning a good enough living to pick up the financial slack for the second two. Without that income, I'd have been back at my desk, episiotomy or not, whenever the paychecks

HOW MUCH TIME WHEN YOU ADOPT?

If you work for a company with fifty or more employees, you're covered by the federal Family and Medical Leave Act—and you can use the twelve-week leave mandated by FMLA to take care of a baby you have just adopted.

The adoption does not even have to be final; according to the National Partnership on Women and Families, your employer is required to give you time off for all the things you have to do to qualify for adoption, including home study visits and court appearances, whether you go through a licensed agency or not. Some states may also require that your company give you a leave to care for an adopted baby, even if you work for a smaller firm. For more information on your rights to leave when you adopt, visit the group's Web site at www.nationalpartnership.org and click on the "supplement" on infertility and adoption.

stopped. I have a feeling I'd have done a pretty good job, too, if I'd had to. Just like all the other women in the world who manage, because they have to. But it's certainly not ideal.

Number two, and just as important, I've come to appreciate just how unique every mom and every new baby is. There's just no magic formula for calculating the perfect maternity leave. It will depend on you, your job, your baby, your spouse, and even what time of year it is. Lock a woman up in a house for the winter in Maine with a colicky baby, no help, and few visitors, and you probably have a woman begging to return to her job—or any job, for that matter. "No one told me how much work a baby would be," says one mom, "how I'd never get anything done all day. I was a mess. My husband suggested I get back to work. He could see I was struggling, and I needed to get some order back in my life." Six weeks after giving birth, this mom was back at work, part-time. "After that, I finally began to enjoy being a mom."

In other cases, it's a matter of personality. Some women, like so many men, just don't like the baby part of parenting. "I loved my work and I was driven," says a senior manager at a bank in Boston. "When I had the second child, I wanted to take off only one month. My boss kept insisting I take more."

But she'd already had a baby, and dreaded being at home for too long. "I kept saying four weeks was fine. He kept insisting I take more. Finally I said to him, 'Can you imagine being a baby, locked up in the house with me for more than four weeks? Me, the hyper one, the impatient one, the one who has to have everything in order and done ahead of time? Me?' He looked at me and said, 'Four weeks sounds about right, doesn't it?' "

But the more typical story goes something like mine. Here's how one of my friends described her first days back at work. "I went back at six weeks and I was so exhausted I couldn't see straight," she says. "Not only that, I missed my baby so much. I just sat in my office and cried the whole first week back at work. I wished I'd had more time."

Three Cardinal Rules

Of course, there's no way to predict in advance what kind of baby you'll have, or how the birth and your recovery will go. Nevertheless, you have to negotiate your maternity leave now. Right now, while you still feel clueless about the whole process of labor, delivery, new babies, and parenthood. So how much time do you ask for? Despite my conviction that all moms and babies are different, I do believe there are three hard and fast rules you should follow. These rules work for anyone and everyone, no matter what your baby, your budget, or your job.

Rule Number One: Ask for the maximum time your employer allows.

Okay, so you may win the baby lottery and get one who sleeps through the night from day one, breastfeeding may go well, and you may be in such terrific shape a few days after the birth that you make the rest of us insanely jealous. And you may have a job that you love, a husband who plans to stay home with the baby, or a great caregiver in the wings. And you're the family breadwinner. So you want to get back to work fast. And when you arrive back on the job at six weeks, you're happy to be there.

All these things could happen. I suppose I've heard that at least five women in America report this situation annually. They are the kind of women who smile and tell their bosses that they really won't need the entire maternity leave off.

But more likely, if you are thinking of asking for less than your employer allows, it's probably for other reasons. You're feeling guilty, for example, for the inconvenience your absence creates on the job, especially if you're due during a busy season at work. Or just because your boss depends on you and wants you back fast. Or because certain customers depend on you, since you know the job better than anyone else does. So you feel guilty, almost like you're taking advantage of your coworkers by taking a leave.

Ignore all those feelings. Ignore your impulse to take care of your boss, your clients, your coworkers. They'll be fine and you'll be back at work before you know it. Everyone will soon forget you were even gone. Honestly.

The bottom line is that it's barbaric that in the United States new moms—and dads—don't have paid parental leave as an automatic benefit. Maternity leave is not a vacation, after all. It is a necessary time for you to recover, get adjusted, learn to care for your new baby, and be ready to function in the world again. The United States retains the dubious distinction of being one of only two industrialized nations in the world not to offer a paid leave (South Africa is the other). By now, most countries, along with all medical authorities, recognize that you need this time off.

Most moms will also tell you that it's hard to leave a tiny baby, especially the first time around. Some women are quite shocked by the depth of the new feelings they have, unlike any others. "I have always loved my job and I just assumed I'd be back at work within six weeks. But once Andrew arrived, everything changed. It wasn't so much that I didn't want to go back to work. I knew I would, eventually. But I wanted to have as much time as I could with him. I just loved being with him, touching those tiny feet, those hands and holding him until he fell asleep," says Stacy, an executive with a small high-tech company. "I immediately extended the leave, so I could just have more time with him."

That is one of the most consistent themes I hear from the hundreds of women I've interviewed over the years. Take every minute your company will give you, paid or unpaid, whatever you can afford and whatever you can cobble together. "It's over so fast, and you never get that time back," says Barbara, a good friend. "I rushed back to work and now it seems so silly. I just wish I'd given myself and Ben another month. At least another month."

If you're not convinced yet that it's wise to ask for as much time as you can get, keep in mind that there are a number of practical problems that can delay your return to work. It can be hard to find child care right away, or the arrangement you make might fall through. You might have a health problem. Your baby might have a health problem. Breastfeeding may not go smoothly. In such situations, it's just no fun to call the boss and ask for an extension of your leave.

Try to imagine it: You're already stressed, facing some new reality that forces you to extend the leave. Even as you dial the number, you remember how your boss or a coworker or one of your friends kept asking you if you were *really* coming back to work at all. Some coworkers and supervisors are probably already predicting that you'll quit. Once you make that call asking for more time, you put your credibility on the line. You've made yourself seem unreliable, far less serious about your job. I've heard the same story over and over again from women: Forget the raise this year, the one you need more than ever, now that you're raising a child. "Many women I know just assume they won't get a bonus or a raise the year they have a baby," says a banker friend of mine. "There was no way that I was going to delay my return by a minute. I had to convince these guys I was totally serious about my work."

Even in nonprofits, my friends tell me, it's better to get the time upfront rather than have to make a request for more time later. Susan, an administrator for a nonprofit agency in the Midwest, remembers the call she had to make. Initially she'd only asked for six weeks, because she worried that a longer absence might cause problems for her employer. But toward the end of maternity leave, she developed a gallbladder problem and had to extend the leave by three weeks. "I think everyone was prepared for me to take a four-to-six-week leave, but not the nine weeks I eventually needed. When I called in and told them I would be out an additional three weeks, my news was not happily received. After my return, I was often teased about how I didn't want to return to work, as if I had 'faked' gallstones in order to have more time off. I was so shocked."

In the end, she concedes, she was naive about the reactions at work. "I suppose I thought everyone would be as excited as I was and not nearly so mean about my absence. Some people actually tried to make me feel guilty about staying home with my son." Within a year of her son's birth, she found a new job.

Hopefully, your coworkers will be more supportive. But rather than risk such treatment, just ask for the maximum leave your employer offers. That gives you more choices and more control over your life in the long run.

If you're still hesitating about this, stop. Remember, you can always ask for *less* time after the baby arrives. This will not create a problem on the job, believe me. If you do get that Buddha baby, or one with colic that drives you back to work, just call the boss and let her know you can't wait to get back. This sort of phone call will instantly transform you into the new heroine of senior management, the new story they like to tell everyone, and most especially other expectant moms. It's the kind of story that goes right along with that mythical vice president of marketing and sales who was signing contracts and closing deals on her way into the delivery room. You'll prove your devotion to the job, dramatically. That's the easy call to make.

So don't sell yourself short up front.

Rule Number Two: Ask for more time.   No matter what the official policy, push for more time if you really want it, can afford to take it, and know it wouldn't jeopardize your job. Four to six months is divine, enough time to recuperate, enjoy the baby, and even get a little bored and ready to do some work again. In a tight labor market, there's very little risk in making such a request. Many employers are willing to cut special deals, to save the expense and time of having to go out and find a replacement for you. Even in a recession, studies show that many companies see "family-friendly" benefits as a way to prop up sagging morale and keep everyone on board.

If your boss is reluctant to be more generous than official policy allows, do some creative thinking about it. Let him know that you'd be willing to stretch the leave by working part-time, sharing a job for a while, or doing some work from home. Many women add vacation, personal, or sick days to the standard leave, or even work holidays or overtime in advance of the birth, to get more time off.

Rule Number Three: Start the leave before the baby is born. Many companies automatically allow women to start maternity leave two weeks before their due date. That's because most doctors recommend this time off, as a standard medical precaution. That time allows you to rest up mentally and physically for the big change ahead. If you're pressed for time, you may not need weeks. But even a few days can help you rest up for labor, and get some quiet moments before your new life begins. "I went out ten days before Andrew was born. It was counted as part of my maternity leave. I know a lot of women don't want to give up time with the baby, but for me, it was really important to have that time before he was born. I'd had an easy pregnancy, but I was tired toward the end, and that time helped me prepare for labor and the sleepless nights that came later," says my friend Laurie, a banker in Boston. "I tell all my friends to do it. It was so good for me."

What's Required by Law?

Okay, so now you are convinced that you should ask for as much time as you can possibly get—and then some. But what, exactly, does your employer *have* to offer you? What's the bare minimum?

There's only one answer to that question, and it's a little complicated.

The answer is that it all depends.

It depends on where you live, where you work, how big your employer is, and what kind of employer you work for. You may be covered by both federal and state laws, which may have different rules about the length of your leave. California's leave law, for example, provides new parents with sixteen weeks off; federal law provides only twelve. You may even be covered by municipal ordinance. In New York City, employers with as few as five workers are subject to the city's Pregnancy Discrimination Ordinance, and they have to give you a disability leave of up to ten weeks.

You may also be covered by no laws at all. You may have to depend on the generosity of your employer.

In general, the bigger your company, the better the policies on maternity leave—and conversely, the smaller the company, the stingier the policies. Few laws require small business people to offer much at all in the way of leave for childbirth.

So how do you know what applies to you? Here are some answers, and ideas on where to turn if you still have questions.

Federal Law:
The Family and Medical Leave Act

If you're pregnant or about to become so, you've probably heard of the Family and Medical Leave Act (FMLA). It took a decade to pass, and President Clinton signed it into law back in 1993, with great fanfare. It's the first such federal law that covers both men and women, and it gives a little better than half of all American workers the right to take up to twelve weeks' off work to care for their newborns or adopted babies. The law also permits workers to take such a leave to care for a seriously ill child or spouse or to recover from their own medical problems.

Prior to the passage of that law, only about a third of all American women had the right to a maternity leave, and usually just six weeks. The rest could be forced to choose between their jobs and caring for their new babies. Under new law, you not only get the time off, but also hang on to your health insurance, with the right to return to your job or an equivalent one at the end of your leave.

But there are catches. The first one concerns the size of the company. The new federal law only covers employers with fifty or more workers. All those fifty employees must have been on the payroll for at least twenty workweeks. Furthermore, you must have fifty coworkers within seventy-five miles of your worksite. This means that if you work at the satellite office for a car-rental agency and the rest of the workers are a hundred miles away, you won't be covered.

Second, you must have been on your employer's payroll for a year before you are eligible for a job-protected leave. During that year, you have to have put in at least 1,250 hours, the equivalent of 25 hours a week for fifty weeks. If you have done these things, and your employer is large enough to be covered by the act, you are entitled to at least twelve weeks off after childbirth or the adoption of a baby, with the right to return to your job or an equivalent one. The leave is unpaid, but health insurance and other benefits must be maintained for you during this time.

There are a few exceptions to these rules. Teachers, for example, are required to take a leave that is not too disruptive to their students. So if you teach and your twelve-week leave ends during the final weeks of an academic year, you may have to wait to return until after the term ends, so the kids can finish up with the teacher who's been in the classroom for most of the term.

Top executives are also subject to special rules. Companies need not provide any leave at all to the most highly paid workers. If you are among the top 10 percent at your firm, you can be denied a leave. "The idea is that the loss of an executive could truly disrupt a business," says Donna Lenhoff, general counsel for the National Partnership on Women and Families and an expert on FMLA. "But employers can't deny the leave willy-nilly. They have to show that keeping the job open [for the woman] would really harm the business."

These days, though, when employers are fighting to keep top talent, it's common for companies to grant a generous leave to executive women to keep them on board. The trade-off is that you'll probably also have to be on call part of the time, by phone, fax, and modem. "I wanted to take four months and I would have liked to have just focused on the baby," says a friend in San Francisco who works for a software company. "But the demands of the job were such that I knew I couldn't be completely gone for the entire time. So I worked out a deal. I got the time at full pay, and I agreed to be on call."

She was lucky on the paycheck. Most women don't get one during their leave, just the guarantee of returning to one after leave—a definite improvement over the bad old days before the federal law was on the books. Prior to passage of FMLA, the only protection most women had was the Pregnancy Discrimination Act, which guaranteed them six weeks off, and only if their employer granted disability leaves at all.

To get the federal leave, you have to follow certain rules. You'll have to give your employer thirty days' advance notice, and you are supposed to give that notice in writing. Once you are ready, it's fairly simple. All you have to do is let your company know that you need the time off to care for a newborn or adopted child. There is no special language or particular phrasing you have to use—just a clear notice of your needs. "There are no magic words you have to use, but it's a good idea to mention FMLA, if it applies. That way, there won't be any confusion later," says Donna Lenhoff.

Many employers require that you have a doctor's note as well, and a growing number of them may also require you to be in touch with a nurse who monitors your leave and your medical condition. "It's all part of a new push to control absences and disability leaves," says Bruce Flynn of Watson and Wyatt Worldwide, a consulting firm based in Washington, D.C., which specializes in human resource issues.

Calculating your time off under this law can be a little tricky. You are clearly entitled to the twelve weeks. But many women hope to extend the time by adding on vacation, sick leave, or any other personal days they have coming. Some employers will let you do that—but they don't have to. Your company can *insist* that you use up all your accrued time off during your leave for childbirth. That comes as a shock to many women who hope to stretch their leaves, or save up those vacation days to use after they get back to work. Instead, they are forced to count them as part of the twelve weeks. "My company told me I had to use up every single vacation day I had, which really upset me. I gave birth in February, and that meant I wouldn't have any more time off for the rest of the year. Not a day in the summer. Even worse,

I knew from friends that I'd want to take some days off after I got back, because the baby would get sick and I'd be going to the doctor," says my friend Maggie. "But the company wouldn't budge. The people in human resources said if they did it for me, then they'd have to do it for everybody and they weren't about to do that."

On the upside, you can take the twelve weeks off in increments, if your boss agrees. You might, for example, return to work half-time for the last two months of your leave, so you don't have to dive back into full-time work right away. My friend Beth worked out an intricate arrangement with her firm that allowed her to add a day a month over a six-month period, so she could come back to work very slowly. "Employers can be as restrictive or as creative as they want to be," says Donna Lenhoff. "The law just guarantees the time off, and leaves it up to you and your company to work out the details."

That Other Federal Law:
The Pregnancy Discrimination Act

If you don't work for a big company, don't despair. You may still be entitled to a leave, albeit a shorter one, under the 1978 Pregnancy Discrimination Act. That law, which covers companies with fifteen or more workers, requires employers to treat pregnant employees the same as a worker disabled by illness or an accident. That means that if disabled workers at your firm—those who suffer a heart attack or break a leg— get a medical leave to recover from their condition, then you are entitled to one as well. If health and retirement benefits continue for those workers on leave, then it must be continued for you as well, while you are on a leave for childbirth.

Under this law, you will most likely get a six-to-eight-week leave, the standard period that doctors certify you need to recover from labor and delivery. As my experience with Daniel shows, it often takes at least a month to six weeks to recover, wake up, get the baby on some sort of schedule, and begin to answer when people start calling you Mom. And by six weeks, this tiny new person might even flash you a smile, reminding you why you wanted to become one.

But all your company will care about is the recovery part. Doctors figure it takes about six weeks for your body to heal, for your hormones to return to normal, and for you to return to your pre-pregnancy self, and that's why the standard medical leave for a vaginal delivery is six weeks. You generally get two more weeks if you have a cesarean. And your doctor may tack on a few more weeks if you have any infections or other health problems connected to childbirth. Your doctor may also extend the period of disability if you have a legitimate medical complication. For example, it may take you a little longer to recover from an episiotomy.

This law does not necessarily require that your company hold your job for you, as the Family and Medical Leave Act does. This law only specifies that you be treated like every other worker with a disability. If they all got their jobs back, then it would be expected that you would as well. "In most cases, you're going to find that a company or a particular boss acts the way you expect them to. If they are generally respectful of employees, then they are going to treat you as well as they can," says Dana Friedman, a national expert on work and family issues and a consultant to many Fortune 500 companies. "If they usually don't treat employees well, then be careful. Those are the places where women tend to have the most problems."

In other words, watch your back. If the only protection you have is the Pregnancy Discrimination Act, and you already know that your company—or your particular boss—tends to treat workers badly, then tread softly. Don't expect your company to suddenly extend you a generous, fully paid leave. Expect to go by the book: Get everything in writing and take notes on all your meetings, to make sure that you are treated fairly.

Some States Give You More Time!

Over the years, many states have passed their own family leave laws that are more generous than the federal laws. Oregon, for example, extends coverage to employers with as few as twenty-five workers. If you live in Washington, D.C., you can take a job-protected leave if you work for a company with only twenty employees. And Vermont requires employers with as few as ten workers to provide time off to care for a newborn or adopted child.

Eight other states extend the time that new moms can take, under some circumstances. In California you can combine a medical leave for childbirth with the twelve-week leave granted under the Family and Medical Leave Act to get up to twenty-eight weeks off in one year to care for a newborn baby or adopted child, and still get your job back. In Rhode Island, you can take up to twenty weeks, if you have a complicated delivery. Louisiana and Tennessee provide four months every year. Connecticut moms can take a four-month job-protected leave every two years. Rhode Island allows thirteen weeks.

This may sound a little better than it is, however. Remember that most of these leaves are unpaid; only five states provide any disability pay at all during a maternity leave and that paycheck is usually a skimpy one—maybe a fraction of your normal paycheck. So you need to think about how much time you can actually afford to take off.

If you want to take the longest leave, you also need to plot out the logistics carefully. You might even want to consult a labor lawyer if you are worried about how you will be treated, just to make sure that you are going to get the time you expect.

Beyond the Law

By now, you've heard of "family-friendly" companies. They make the lists of national magazines, get loads of publicity, and leave many of us salivating for jobs with them. They offer job sharing, professional part-time work, and telecommuting, and they promote women, even women who choose to work less than 100 hours a week. Even better, they promote dads who work less than 100 hours a week, signaling to all of us that they really *are* family-friendly.

These companies offer the best maternity leaves in the world. IBM, for example, allows women to take up to three *years*, with a guarantee that you will return to a job comparable to the one you left before you had a child. A good chunk of the first six months may also come with a paycheck. The accounting firm of Ernst and Young offers up to seventy-two weeks of parental leave. Johnson & Johnson, Eli Lilly, Lincoln Financial Group, Procter & Gamble, and Sears, Roebuck all offer a year or more. What these rare employers have discovered is that treating employees well helps their bottom line. Even a minor improvement in maternity benefits can provide a big bang for the bucks. Aetna, for example, figured that it saved nearly $2 million back when it extended leaves by an extra four weeks. How? Women stopped leaving the company—so the insurance giant no longer had to waste money recruiting and training replacements. IBM found that family-friendly benefits ranked second only to salary as a reason for staying with Big Blue among its highest-achieving employees.

A few employers now even offer a paid paternity leave to encourage dads to spend time caring for their new babies.

Certainly, there's nothing to stop your employer from being more generous than the law allows. "We always try to remind both employers and women that the law only spells out a floor," says Donna Lenhoff. "Companies can always do more, and those that do often find it benefits them."

It would be nice to believe that employers of the future will all come to that conclusion. In the meantime, you have to deal with reality. The reality for most American women is that they can expect at least six weeks at most companies— and maybe even three months at a decent-sized firm.

But once you understand the time off you're going to get, you begin to see there's this other problem looming. "What most women don't realize is that all leaves from employment are just about time off, not about pay," says Ray Werntz of the Employee Benefit Research Institute.

In other words, most employers, when they talk about leave, are not talking about paid leave at all. That's not on their agenda. In fact, the last time I checked, the nation's largest corporations had hired a cadre of lobbyists to show up on Capitol Hill and oppose any law that might force them to offer paid leave.

So once you figure out how much time your employer must give you—and even how much time your employer *will* give you—you have to move on to the next question: How much money can you collect while you're out on leave?

It's a question that creeps in, colors everything and may finally determine how much time off you request. Although you may find that this question only occurs to you late in the game, after you are pregnant. Maybe even after you are on leave, if you're as crazy as I was.

Chapter 2

Show Me the Money

*I*f I slept most of the time after Dan, it was quite the opposite with Rachel, my first child. After her birth, I don't remember sleeping at all. Instead, I was awake and anxious. I used every moment she slept to fix her room, wash the dishes, clean the house, wash her clothes, and call friends. I even made curtains for her room. Me, the one who hadn't sewn a stitch since middle school. New-mommy-itis took over and kept me busy. I was creating a nursery, a new life, and a new home. Thank god Martha Stewart hadn't launched her empire yet. I would probably have been bronzing Rachel's baby slippers, or making candles for her room.

Nearly everyone told me not to behave this way. But I ignored them and just kept moving.

Oh, and I worried. Worrying took up gobs of time.

Not having a paycheck for that maternity leave was a big source of the worry, sending me into periodic panics about our finances then—and well into the future. There was the day when Rachel was just a few months old, and I decided I was in urgent need of my first life insurance policy. Up until that morning, the need for life insurance had never seemed particularly pressing. But that morning it seemed incredibly irresponsible that I hadn't invested in life insurance eons ago. How could I go another day? How could my family survive without that policy? What if something happened to me?

The new anxiety drove me to stuff Rachel into the Snugli and march eight blocks in ankle-deep snow to my neighborhood bank. All the way there, I worried that I might get hit by a car before I arrived and secured said policy and knew that Rachel's financial future was assured. Once at the bank, a perfectly pleasant manager informed me it would take at least a few days to process the new policy. He seemed to think I'd survive the wait.

His impervious calm momentarily deflated my anxiety. I could even laugh at myself. I wasn't going to die soon! This was not urgent!

Yet spending money on new baby clothes, diapers, wipes, and all the rest reminded me that we had new expenses that came with our new responsibilities. And they were only likely to grow. Now it was an infant seat, but soon it would be a high chair, a bed, even a new room for Rachel. We were still living in an apartment, with only four rooms. We'd have to move, eventually. Thinking about the future often dominated the present. I couldn't fall asleep on a couch, much less a concrete floor. I was AWAKE. And, as much as I tried to push the thought away, I knew I needed to get back to work fast.

After Dan, I didn't feel that way. I was relaxed because I had a paycheck coming in, and a good job waiting for me. I see now, as I contrast the two maternity leaves, that the paycheck during the second gave us not only a financial cushion but also some emotional space, some time to adapt to the enormous change in our lives.

So now I tell all my friends, whatever you do, make sure you plan out the money part. Or at least try to. The smart ones have already figured this out. "I know some people romanticize skimping after the baby is born," says my friend Lisa. "But not me. I knew that if I wasn't working, we'd be living paycheck to paycheck or worse. I didn't want that kind of stress. After a baby, you're working through a lot of emotions anyway and adding financial stress to everything else would have been too much for us."

Figure It Out Now

Sound advice, but most of us leap before we look. We get so excited at the prospect of that tiny new baby entering our lives that we ignore the practicalities, never consulting that company benefits book until we are already pregnant and uncertain how we can afford to take even five minutes off work after the baby arrives. And when we do wake up and pay attention, lots of us are plenty shocked to learn that while we may get some time off, there's often no paycheck at all aside from the vacation time or sick leave that we've earned in the past year. Or a disability check that is a pittance compared to regular pay. "Oh, I got state disability checks, all right. But that didn't amount to much," says my friend Ellen. "I can't even remember how much it was now. It was so little. Maybe a hundred dollars a week. I was shocked. I had just assumed I'd get a paycheck when I went on leave. After all, I knew my job was protected, so I figured I'd get a check, too. How else can a family survive?"

A good question, and one that this country has yet to answer in a very satisfactory way. For the most part, you are at the mercy of your employer's generosity, or lack of it. Most women piece together a combination of short-term disability payments, sick time, vacation days, and personal leave, if they have it, to stretch their leave as long as they possibly can and maximize the amount of money coming in. "I worked every holiday within that eight-month period after I learned I was pregnant to get more time off later," says Amy, a medical technologist in Kentucky. "And I took advantage of my hospital's policy that allowed me to convert sick leave into vacation pay. By the time I was ready for maternity leave, I had saved enough time to take a twelve-week paid leave." Her story is a common one, except that the amount of time she managed to piece together is not typical. Many employers don't allow workers to carry over so much sick leave, and may even limit the vacation time you can take in a year. And most workers can't accrue so much time during their pregnancies, or even a year! Outside of holidays, the average American worker has only about three weeks of paid time off a year, a combination of sick days, vacation, and personal leave.

So what, exactly, can you expect? How will you manage? Here's the rundown on possible sources of income.

Disability Compensation

Disability Pay from Your Company

Federal and state laws do guarantee a little more than half of us the right to take some time off, but those laws do not address pay at all. "A lot of women are surprised by this. They say, 'I'm on leave, I'm entitled to that by law. So I should get money, too,'" says Ray Werntz of the Employee Benefits Research Institute (EBRI) in Washington. "But that's not how it works. Employers see a leave of absence as a privilege they grant the employee, or a right if it's required by law. It's just a way of saying, 'I like you enough that I want you to come back.'

"But that is separate from the money. If you know you're going to need money for maternity leave, it's a good idea to see what kind of sick leave or short-term disability plan your employer offers," he says. "I'd do that even before I took a job with a company."

In fact, apart from pay for the vacation and sick time you have saved up, a disability check is probably the only one you'll see during maternity leave. Though not required by law, most employers do carry disability insurance—about two thirds of them, at last count. That's important, because for employment purposes, you are considered medically disabled by pregnancy and childbirth. And these plans usually have some form of "salary replacement" available to disabled workers. That's a fancy way of saying that the insurance company agrees to provide you with some sort of income while you recover and get ready to come back to work. It's the same benefit extended to workers who suffer a heart attack or some other medical emergency that keeps them off the job.

In the case of pregnancy and childbirth, you are typically considered disabled for two weeks before your due date and six to eight weeks after the birth—six for a normal vaginal delivery and eight for a cesarean. If you do have complications during birth or afterward—an infection, trouble with the healing of the episiotomy—your doctor or the nurse from the insurance company may certify that you are disabled for a longer period, which keeps the checks coming.

So far, so good, you say. It means *some* cash will be coming in. But hang on, girls. There are many catches in this system.

For starters, there's usually a waiting period for these checks to start, anywhere from a few days to an entire month. And in many cases, your employer may require you to use up your sick days, personal time, and vacation before the disability checks begin. My friend Isabel had to weather an entire month before she saw a single check from the insurance company. "Maternity here falls under short-term disability, which doesn't start until the thirty-first day you are out. Employees are expected, during the first thirty days of leave, to use all their available sick and annual leave accrued to date. If on the thirty-first day you are still unable to return to work, your pay continues at either one hundred percent or fifty percent, depending on years of service," she says. "In my case, after my initial thirty-day wait, my pay did continue at one hundred percent, which was a godsend." But, of course, it only lasted another two weeks, taking her up to the sixth week after the baby was born.

In most cases, the paycheck supplied by private disability insurance is less than your normal one. "The idea is to help people out, but to also make sure it is attractive for them to return to work. You don't want to be so generous that people don't want to come back to work. That's why the typical insurance policy or leave benefit plan replaces only a percentage of salary, usually fifty to seventy percent of salary. I'd say about ninety percent of the policies are in that range," says Bruce Flynn of Watson and Wyatt Worldwide, a Washington, D.C., management consulting firm that specializes in human resources issues.

The amount you collect is often pegged to your seniority and job rank: The longer you've been with your company and the more senior you are, the more likely you are to get a full paycheck for at least part of your leave. "A rule of thumb is that most employers provide two thirds to three fourths of pay during the time you are disabled. But some employers have plans customized to meet their needs, so they offer more help to the workers they consider to be the most valuable," says Ray Werntz from EBRI. "These plans are all over the lot, so you just have to ask and find out what your employer provides."

Exact figures are hard to come by, but one federal study shows your chances of getting full pay at any time during maternity leave are about one in four. The prospects of a partial paycheck are much higher—about 60 percent of women on leave get partial pay. The way that those checks arrive can seem bizarre—you may get larger checks at the beginning of your leave—even full pay—and then have the checks disappear altogether by the time your disability period ends. "I got full pay for the first three weeks, and then nothing," says one woman. "I'd only worked for the company for three years. If I'd been here for five years, I could have collected six weeks of full pay."

Another friend in the Midwest reports that her employer's disability plan paid 75 percent of her paycheck while she was out. My pal Lucy, also in the Midwest but at a smaller firm, said disability there was just 55 percent of her paycheck.

Even getting a partial paycheck is a relatively new benefit in the United States. Prior to the mid-1970s, women were simply expected to quit their jobs and go home, whether they needed the money or not. It was the Pregnancy Discrimination Act, passed in 1978, that finally spurred many employers to offer some sort of salary replacement. All employers with fifteen or more employees are now required to treat a woman who has had a baby the same as any other disabled worker.

Bottom line? If you've worked awhile in middle management for a large corporation, you're probably going to do okay. You may even find yourself eligible for several months of fully paid leave. This is uncommon, but it does happen. My friend Amy, who works as a manager for a big oil company, got six weeks at full pay plus another six months at half pay. Not only that, she could collect state disability payments once she moved to half pay. "I have very good benefits and the company treats those on maternity leave well," she says. No kidding!

State Disability Checks

Five states—New Jersey, New York, California, Hawaii, and Rhode Island—require that all employers buy disability policies that cover pregnancy and childbirth. So if you live in one of those states, you are guaranteed a check during maternity leave, though it rarely matches the one you regularly bring home from work, especially if you are making a decent salary. State disability payments are awarded on a sliding scale, depending on your salary, but they do have a ceiling. In California, for example, the ceiling is $336 a week, and most women get far less. The average payment is just $229 a week. "My company's policy is to allow up to six months of unpaid leave. But here in California, the disability pay is so low that it makes it very difficult to take that much time off, especially if you are in a high-income position," says Ruth, a marketing executive who works for a mid-sized company in Northern California. A friend of hers decided to sock away $100 a month during her pregnancy when she found out she'd only get $178 a week under the California plan. Diane, a friend who lives and works in New York City, has three words for the $187 a week she got from the state during her leave. "What a joke!" "How could anyone live on that, especially with a baby!" She used up her sick and vacation time to make ends meet.

Nevertheless, for those of us who need every penny we can get after the baby is born, these benefits can make a critical difference. The average benefit collected in New Jersey was $273 a week; in Hawaii, it was $275. New York, despite its high standard of living, offered the lowest benefit—a maximum of $170 a week.

Whatever the amount, these benefits will usually arrive in the form of a check from the state and only keep coming while the doctor certifies you are disabled. For most of us, that is just six weeks for a vaginal delivery and eight for a cesarean. Many employers do supplement the state payments with their own—the fact that your state may have a statewide disability insurance system doesn't stop your employer from being more generous. When I had Daniel my company guaranteed full pay for eight weeks, even though New York State offered a check as well. My firm did ask me to sign the state disability checks over to them, since they were paying my full salary too. "Most employers do have protections to keep employees from double-dipping! It's not unusual for them to have some provision in place to make sure that you don't collect more from disability than you would from your normal paycheck," says consultant Flynn from Watson and Wyatt Worldwide.

A shame, if you ask me. The truth is that other countries offer new moms not only disability pay, but health insurance, free health care for the new baby, *plus* a family allowance. In France, all women get sixteen weeks at full pay; women in Chile get a full paycheck for up to eighteen weeks. "You have to feel sorry for the American working mother," says Sheila Kamerman, a professor of social work at Columbia University and an expert on family-friendly policies around the world. "Most countries recognize not only that women need some pay while on leave, but that it costs a lot to raise children and it's in the country's interest to help families get off to a good start."

Union benefits

If you work under a union contract you may be in luck. Membership in a union is one of the best predictors of being able to afford to take a maternity leave without running up your credit cards, emptying the piggybank, or going on welfare. In fact, a growing number of union contracts now include parental leave benefits, including some pay, even for dads and adoptive parents. The clerical workers union at Harvard University won thirteen weeks of maternity leave, with most of it at full pay. Adoptive parents and dads are also eligible for four weeks of paid leave. Employees of the state of Ohio recently won four weeks of paid leave for either birth or adoption.

Yet such agreements are still rare. "There's certainly more attention to the need for better leave policies, and to have some pay during leave," says Netsy Firestein, who monitors union agreements on family issues for the Labor Project for Working Families. "But it's still hard to find examples of extended, full pay during maternity leave."

Her own organization is one of those few great examples: Fully-paid leave for sixteen weeks for moms, dads, and adoptive parents.

Ahead of the Pack

Some good-guy employers have come to realize that a decent maternity leave makes good business sense. Most of them are in industries such as high technology, drugs, and communications that have had to compete mightily for qualified new workers—and this has spurred them to figure out new perks to gain that competitive edge. IBM, for example, was one of the first companies in America to offer a fully paid leave for eight weeks or longer as well as the option to return to work part-time—along with a job guarantee of up to several years. These days, as previously noted, Big Blue is allowing paychecks that may last for much longer than eight weeks and leaves of up to three years.

Not surprisingly, employees are enthusiastic about such family-friendly treatment. Johnson & Johnson and other pharmaceutical companies offer a range of perks, including on-site child care and paid leaves, to get the best workers. "They were competing for the best talent in a very tight labor market," says the consultant Dana Friedman. "It was the best way to make sure that they could get the people to help them create the best products and compete in the marketplace."

In the recent economic boom, more and more employers scrambled to make themselves the employer of choice, offering better and better leave policies and help with child care. Chase Manhattan Bank began to offer not only a fully paid leave of up to eight weeks but also free child care for new infants and a part-time return to work for new moms who want it. "The benefits are so good here that it's hard to even think about leaving," says Diana, a manager who has stayed with the bank for thirteen years. "Everything about my leave was made easy. It was just one phone call and my managers did all the paperwork, and then I had the time, the pay, and even child care free for three months. What could be better?"

Health Insurance and Other Benefits

Of course, a paycheck may not be the only reason why your job is essential to your family. Many of us work today to ensure the family has health insurance—and on this front, you probably don't have to worry while on leave. If you are covered by the Family and Medical Leave Act, your employer must continue to pay for your health benefits for the entire leave, up to twelve weeks. The terms of the coverage continue just as they would if you were sitting at your desk. If you usually pay part of the premium, you'll have to continue to do so during your leave. If not, your company will continue to pick up the tab.

If you are not covered by the Family and Medical Leave Act, you may still have legal protection of your health insurance under the Pregnancy Discrimination Act. That law, which covers employers with as few as fifteen employees, specifies that your health insurance policy must continue during your disability period and that coverage for your spouse must continue as well. That period may be much shorter than the one granted under FMLA—only six weeks in many cases—but it can be a big help. And in the worst-case scenario, most employers will let you pay the premium to keep the insurance going until you get back to work.

Under the federal law, the rest of your benefit package is basically frozen in place while you are on leave, including retirement, disability, and any other perks you now receive as part of your regular compensation. Your 40l(k) or other pension plan simply continues to accrue its normal gains or losses, as it would when you are on the job, but your company does not have to keep contributing to retirement plans while you are on leave. Some will do it, so it's good to ask, even if it's not formal policy. But the law does not require it. All the law specifies is that your employer cannot discontinue any benefits while you are on leave.

You also retain your seniority while you are out on leave. That's the good news. The bad news is that you don't accrue any further credits toward seniority while you are out. In other words, you are stopped in time—you don't lose anything, but you don't gain anything on this front, either.

Adoption

If you're in the process of adopting a baby, much of this chapter may be frustrating to you! If you are covered by a state or federal law which grants a leave, at least you have time with your baby, even if no paycheck. But your bank account may be hurting, since most pay flows from employers' disability plans and you do not qualify as a disabled worker. God knows you may feel like one, after waking for night feedings. "No one can describe to you how tiring it is, how demanding it is. I wouldn't trade it for the world, but I never thought I'd ever get enough sleep again," says Emily, one weary mom who adopted. "And unlike all my friends who'd been through the pregnancy and were somewhat prepared to dive in, we just got a call from the adoption agency, and suddenly, we felt like we were under siege, sleepwalkers trying to care for this baby." And, she adds, "We'd just about run through our savings, just paying for the adoption. That cost us well over ten thousand dollars before we got everything settled. So I couldn't afford to go too long without a paycheck."

Her solution? Like so many women, she got back to work two weeks after the baby came home, far sooner than she'd wished. Did she have a choice? Is there any hope for adoptive parents?

The answer is, a little, even if it is a very little. Some companies now offer both cash to ease the pain of the adoption process and a paycheck along with leave for a while after the baby arrives. They recognize that such a benefit helps workers adjust and come back ready to do a good job, helps attract top talent to their ranks, and helps stem turnover. Several Fortune 500 companies, including IBM, Merck, and Johnson & Johnson, offer workers thousands of dollars to help defray the cost of adoption. In addition, firms such as Chase Manhattan Bank offer at least some paid time to adoptive parents.

Some unions have also been active on behalf of adoptive parents. As noted, Harvard University's clerical union offers adoptive parents eight weeks of paid leave. But this is a recent and rare bargain for an employer to strike with its union.

Paternity Leave

Yes, a few companies in America recognize that more dads would stay home with a new baby if only they had a paycheck coming in. Lotus began offering fathers eight weeks' paid leave in the mid–1990's, and dads jumped on the bandwagon. More than one hundred took advantage of the leave in one year alone.

But the sad truth is that child care is still regarded as women's work, even women's sacred duty. So most firms simply feel no pressure to offer men any pay to be home with their new baby. The fact that maternity leave is largely defined as a period of disability in this country also leaves men out. The Family and Medical Leave Act was one of the first laws in any developed country to recognize that men are parents too. Still, no paycheck is attached to that leave.

Getting the Skinny

How do you find out what your company offers? The first thing many people will tell you is to run down to personnel or human resources and ask about maternity leave. Or they'll tell you to consult your company's benefit book. Those are great ideas in the abstract. But at many companies, the maternity leave policy—and especially the money part—is not spelled out in detail anywhere. And even when you do find references to it in the company benefits book, the description may be hard to follow. Even experts concede that the same folks who write the instruction manuals for self-assemble gas grills or Ikea's bunk beds probably pen most of these insurance policies.

Whatever you do, make your preliminary queries discreetly. Your best bet is to consult someone in human resources whom you know you can trust to keep things confidential, or just sit down and have a heart-to-heart with another mom who just took a leave. Discretion is important in these preliminary sessions because once your boss gets wind that you're pregnant, he or she may start pressing you about your plans—and it's really a mistake to talk to anyone official about your leave until you are clear about what you want in terms of time off, workload, and pay.

Whoever you consult, you'll want to get some answers to these basic questions. What you find out will help you shape the request you make to your firm, both in terms of time and money.

Is there a paid leave that is separate from any disability insurance plan?

If so, how many weeks will you get, and at what rate of pay? Does the rate of pay vary with your years of service? Are you still eligible if you just started the job this calendar year? Are any employees exempt from the plan? Top managers are not covered by the Family and Medical Leave Act—the assumption is that they are so valuable that the company would be hard-pressed to do without them even for twelve weeks.

If paychecks come through the disability plan, is there a waiting period before they start?

If so, you may need to plan on using your vacation time or sick or personal days to make ends meet until the insurance payments kick in. In fact, your company may *require* you to do so. "At my company, the short-term disability doesn't kick in until the tenth day of leave. So before that, it is considered regular sick time," says one mom. "The trouble with that is that my company didn't let me carry over much sick or vacation time from year to year—so this put me in a financial pinch. I finally decided I couldn't take as much time as I wanted, because of those ten days without pay."

Does the doctor determine when the disability checks stop?

One mom ended up having to repay the insurance company for a check she got while on leave, because of her doctor's timing. "One thing I wasn't expecting was that my doctor was going to be out of town at the time when my six-week checkup would have fallen, after the baby was born. So the doctor's office asked me to come in earlier, just short of five weeks. That was fine with me," she recalls. "But what I didn't realize was that when my doctor filed with the disability insurance that I was medically okay to return to work, that ended my disability payments—and it was earlier than I had planned.

"In fact, since they had already mailed me a disability check, I then had to refund the insurance company for just over a week, which was not fun to do at a time when money was the tightest it's ever been! If I had known this would happen, I would have waited until *after* his vacation to have my appointment. But that was about the only problem with my leave."

Will a nurse from the disability insurance company monitor your progress during recovery after childbirth?

If so, this can also affect how long you collect a paycheck. "My Kemper [the insurance agency] nurse called me weekly to check my progress," says another mom. "On paper my company would allow up to twenty weeks off for a pregnancy with some complications. But she followed my progress every week, and checked in with my doctor as well. At eight weeks, my doctor released me and that was the end of my checks."

Does the amount of disability payment vary, depending on your years of service or depending on the length of your disability?

Many insurance plans are set up in such a way that the size of the checks diminishes over time, or the checks disappear altogether, to encourage you to get back to work. But the benefit is more generous the longer you have worked for the company. Benefits vary in this way because companies are trying to balance ways to retain you—but not to let you stay at home with a generous check for too long.

If you live in one of the five states with temporary disability insurance, what is the maximum amount you can collect? For how long? Will your company supplement that check?

Many small employers will expect you to get along on the meager checks from the state disability insurance. But larger companies often kick in some extra money to help you maintain something closer to your normal income.

Is there a limit on the number of paid personal, vacation, or sick days that you can apply toward your leave?

Answers to this question can vary widely—and can make an enormous difference in your planning, judging by the experience of my friends. "I was startled to learn that I couldn't use more than two weeks' vacation time in a year," says my friend Marcy. "I had saved up some days, starting right when I got pregnant, thinking I could use them on leave. But then I was told that no one is able to use more than three weeks in a year."

Compare that to the experience of my friend Linda, a paralegal for a law firm in Boston, who'd been with the firm for fourteen years before she had her first child. "I've always enjoyed working and I didn't even realize that I was accumulating so many personal days. But by the time I was ready to have the baby, I discovered I had three hundred days, which allowed me to be compensated one hundred percent for my entire maternity leave. I was thrilled!"

Can you use comp time to stretch out your leave?

Again, it's smart to find out the details and not make any assumptions. My friend Sarah just assumed she could use some of her comp time to extend her leave and make it easy on the family budget. But no such luck. "I work at a small ad agency, and comp time is allowed for many things," she says. "The comp time plan allowed staff members to take time off on a matching basis for overtime put in. I had witnessed this time being used by other male and female members for a variety of reasons and planned to use some for my maternity leave. In fact, I thought I could plan to create more comp time during my pregnancy by working overtime. But when I met with management to walk through my plan for the leave of absence for maternity, to my surprise, management told me they had a concern about offering comp time for maternity leave. The discussion became quite heated."

She was lucky enough to have a manager who supported her, and suggested that management consult legal counsel before denying her request. The firm's lawyer advised them to grant her request; a denial for maternity leave could be interpreted as discrimination against women. So her request was granted. Yet the agency subsequently changed its policy on comp time, limiting its use in relation to maternity leave and a number of other situations. "I was so upset. It was a small firm, and everyone knew why they did it. There was a lot of resentment toward me, for the restrictions on the use of comp time. I ended up finding another job and leaving the firm."

Is there a pool of time or pay that all employees contribute to that you can draw on in a pinch?

A growing number of workplaces—especially government workplaces—have created a pool of leave time that employees can share. The idea is that some workers simply won't use their sick leave or personal days in a particular year—or at least not all of them—and they can donate the time to coworkers facing tough situations. In many cases, colleagues donate the time to help out workers who need time off to care for a child or a spouse with a serious illness. The good news is that you may be able to tap such a pool for your maternity leave. "I'm a single mom," said Suzanne, who worked for the state of California, "and we had no official, paid maternity leave at my state job. We are supposed to use up our vacation and sick leave. But I ended up on bed rest for six weeks during my second trimester, and used up all my vacation and sick leave then. The saving grace for me was that other government workers could donate days to me. I got seventeen days of donated leave from friends, coworkers and even strangers. It saved my life!"

Making It Work

So where does this leave you? Once you understand the policies and get answers to the above questions, you will understand why so many of us end up patching together whatever sick days, vacation time, and personal leave we can to make ends meet while out on leave. It's no wonder that no two experiences are the same, even at the same company.

Look at the variety of approaches used by three of my friends.

An administrator at a Midwestern college: "I used twenty-two days of personal time and thirteen sick days plus disability pay to get through eight weeks at basically full pay."

A manager for United Way in Ohio: "I used ten days of carried-over vacation, plus one holiday and one new vacation day. That, plus extended sick leave got me through my leave. My doctor extended my period of disability because I had low iron at my six-week checkup. So I got my sick leave extended beyond the usual six weeks."

A middle manager at a drug company in New Jersey: "I got six months at full pay, plus I had on-site day care when I came back to work. During my leave, I got one check from New Jersey, and another from my company that made up the difference in my paycheck."

So you need to tally up what you have available, the rules at your company and in your state that govern the time and pay you can get—and then decide what to bargain for. As you sort out what you want, however, do add in a couple of other considerations.

Don't be too quick to use up all your sick leave, personal days, and vacation during maternity leave. Chances are you're going to need them after you get back to work. Babies get sick, you'll get sick, and you'll need to go to the pediatrician frequently the first year, if only for well-baby visits. And God knows, you'll find that both you and your husband will long for a vacation, if only an extended weekend, once everything settles down.

Most likely your company will offer you more unpaid than paid time and will expect you to fill your pocketbook as best you can during the unpaid time you take. That may mean cashing in savings bonds, as one of my friends did. Or even borrowing money from family. But don't ever assume that you can't get what you want and need.

When it comes to any aspect of your maternity leave, try to remember, when you run into resistance, that everything is negotiable—and it doesn't hurt to ask for what you want. The executive of one software company in San Francisco recently negotiated a month at full pay and several months of part-time work from home, even though the firm had just laid off a third of its staff and there was no formal policy or law that protected her. "I went before the board and told them that I would be available by phone and e-mail, and I would not drop any balls," she says. "But if I did not get a leave, and get a paid leave, I did not see how I could continue to work for the company." They gave her what she asked for.

PAID LEAVE: ON THE HORIZON?

Some twenty states are now considering bills that would create a paid parental leave, so you wouldn't have to take such a financial hit when you stay home with your new baby. In most cases, state lawmakers are looking into ways to use unemployment insurance to create a paid leave, the method many other countries use to create a paycheck for new parents out on leave.

"We're really excited about the quick action and progress that's being made toward creating a paid leave," says Donna Lenhoff of the National Partnership for Women and Families, which is spearheading the movement.

To find out what's going on in your state, or to join those lobbying for paid leave, visit the group's Web site at www.nationalpartnership.org.

WHERE DO WOMEN HAVE IT BETTER?

When it comes to maternity leave, women in just about every other developed country get a better deal than we do. Just look at policies in these countries:

Chile	18 weeks	100% of pay
France	16 weeks	100% of pay
Germany	14 weeks	100% of pay
Italy	20 weeks	100% of pay
Norway	52 weeks	80% of pay

(SOURCE: Sheila Kamerman, "From Parenting to Maternity Policies: Women's Health, Employment and Child and Family Well-being.")

Chapter 3

Selling the Boss:
Are You Really Coming Back?

A week before Daniel was born, I sat at work in the midst of one of the best baby showers ever. About fifteen of us were gathered in the company dining room, plates piled high with food, gabbing and laughing, taking inventory of a table loaded with gifts. My coworkers oohed and ahed as I opened each present. There were the tiny cotton pajamas, knit hats, booties, blankets, and all the rest. Clint, a colleague with a flair for the dramatic, took ribbons from each gift, wove them together, taped them on a paper plate and created the perfect, ridiculous crown for my pregnant body.

I was one of four pregnant women in the office at the time, and we freely shared our anxieties and joy, openly cavorting in the office. We even mounted Polaroid snapshots on the wall, chronicling the progress of our ballooning bodies. No one scolded us or looked askance. The whole mood of the office was festive.

A workplace like this obviously makes it easy to negotiate maternity leave. In fact, when I told my boss I was pregnant, she clapped her hands and was nearly as excited as I was. She knew I'd waited for this pregnancy for a while. Company policy was generous and clear. Four months off, with two at full pay. What could be better?

I've heard stories from other friends who work in equally warm and friendly workplaces, where baby showers are the norm and women come by to show off their babies during maternity leave.

But such employers may still be the exception. Even though we've entered the new millennium, plenty of bosses still live in the dark ages, and immediately assume that if you're pregnant, you're going to stop working the minute the baby arrives. Even the enlightened ones may begin to worry about your absence. Most companies still don't plan out how the work will get done while you're out, so your boss is left holding the bag. Though she may want to be happy for you, she also has to be asking herself, "What will this cost me? When is she coming back? *Is* she coming back? How's the work going to get done?"

"My news was greeted with a kind of uncomfortable, hushed silence. I think my boss was flustered, and then worried about what this meant for him, for the company," says my friend Martha. "He didn't say it at the time, but I gathered from our conversations later that he just assumed I wouldn't come back after the baby was born."

Other friends have endured true Neanderthals. One boss advised a woman I know to get an abortion if she ever got pregnant. Another was greeted with a simple expletive when she announced her news. "All he said was 'Shit!," she recalls. "That's it. The only word that came out of his mouth."

Others are just clueless. Take the men who work with my friend Arlene at a diesel engine manufacturing plant in Virginia. "I was the only woman working in sales at the time, and the men that I worked with honestly did not believe me when I stated I was coming back to work," she says. She set herself up with a computer at home, had her mail delivered at home once a week, and managed to keep up with things during her eight weeks "off."

Many bosses like Arlene's are well-intentioned, but baffled by pregnancy. They'd like to be supportive, if only they knew how. If only they didn't have to worry about how to get the work done; if only a maternity leave didn't disrupt their routines and schedules.

That's why your first step in negotiating is to baby the boss. Don't assume that he shares your joy, wants to take care of you, or even believes that you are coming back. Instead, think of him as a child who you must coddle and cajole to get the leave you want.

Milk the Grapevine

To do that, you've got to learn to see things through his eyes. If he's going to grant you a generous leave, he's going to have to justify it. If he's going to grant you a more generous leave than most, he's going to have to justify that as well. If he's not very creative to start with, you're going to have to give him some creative arguments. Do his homework for him.

Start by finding out exactly what kind of leaves the company has granted recently and how they went. And I'm not talking about just what's on paper in the company benefits book.

If you've gotten answers to all the questions I suggested in the last chapter, you know what other women in your company have really gotten and how their leaves went. These days, the most valued workers are cutting sweeter deals, winning more time, a flexible return to work, and, sometimes, even more money. No one broadcasts these deals. "No one likes to talk about it, and leaves shouldn't be granted on grounds of merit. Everyone needs them. But in practice, companies tend to do more for the ones they see as the most valuable," says Dana Friedman, a longtime consultant on work and family issues in corporate America. It's also common for bosses to ask that such deals be kept quiet, to stop everyone from clamoring for better treatment.

So start asking around, and find out what other women have recently negotiated. Once you connect to the grapevine, you'll learn a lot about which bosses, which departments, which divisions are the most family-friendly. Your search may also lead you to an incredibly valuable source and new pal. Nothing makes women closer than talking about pregnancy, the new baby, and maternity leave. You may instantly win a new best friend who can help you prepare your case. She'll know what's important and what to forget about. "I was worried sick about how my paperwork would get done while I was out," says one friend. "But Emily told me the boss didn't care about that at all. Not that I shouldn't get it done. But she said what I should emphasize to him was how I'd keep in touch with our clients; be available by phone, fax, and e-mail, if I could be."

Just as important, your detective work will reveal what kind of act you're following—and that can make or break your case. If your boss just granted generous leaves to three women who quit two days before they were due back at work, you're going to have to do a lot of swimming upstream to get what you want. Of course, if three or four women just came back ahead of time, enthusiastic, and productive, you're likely to hit no resistance at all.

Whatever the situation, don't get too cocky. There are so many variables that your boss must consider, and you have to try to anticipate all of them. Even the way the economy is going, or your particular industry. Think about the context of the sweetest deals you've found out about—those four- or five-month leaves at full pay, for example. Were they granted in the midst of the dot.com boom? If so, be prepared for your boss to feel differently in the face of rising oil prices and predictions of recession right around the corner. The labor shortage of the 1990s grew so acute that firms were falling all over themselves to be "family-friendly." But that attitude can change as quickly as a dot.com can go belly up. If the firm just announced a hiring freeze or started handing out the pink slips, take that into account. "I wouldn't give up on what you want, but if the economy slows down, I wouldn't shoot the moon the way I would in a great economy," says Friedman.

Finally, know what you're worth—face it, bringing in big bucks is mostly what counts. A few years ago, I interviewed one of the most successful moms on Wall Street, Susan Schnerbel, a managing director at Merrill Lynch. Susan had it good and she knew it. Once she had kids, she cut a deal to work from home and show up in the office only when her presence was absolutely essential. Her secret? "I'd like to think they'd let me do this even if I did the same work as everyone else. But I wouldn't bet my mortgage on that. I have a valuable specialty that no one else has—no one at Merrill Lynch, and hardly anyone else even on Wall Street." With a background in tax benefits, she can help firms figure out the tax consequences of employee benefit plans as well as corporate taxes when firms merge or buy each other out.

Ann, a professor of biology at a large and prestigious university, wanted to take the full three-month maternity leave her institution—on paper—says it allows. She knew that wasn't going to sit well with some of her colleagues, who were mostly men. "Nobody liked the idea of your being away from your lab that long," she says. "No one said it directly, but you could read it in their body language."

But bringing in the bucks turned things around. "I got a big grant the first day I went out on leave, and the second week, I got another grant! I was batting a thousand, so that shut everybody up!" she says.

Making Your Case

Okay, you've got the big picture. You know what you're worth, what the formal policies are, and what other women have been getting lately. Now all you have to do is decide exactly what you want, and make the case for it.

Three months at full pay?

Six months?

A year?

Let's see, what you want is a raise, two years at full pay, benefits, and extra contributions to your 401(k). Plus full-time help for the first three months and an all-expenses-paid vacation to Hawaii when you and your hubby are ready. That's what you *want*.

You also hope to win the lottery tomorrow.

Realistically, you think you might get two or three months with pay, and another month using your saved-up vacation time and raiding the family cookie jar. At least, that's what you'd like, and what you believe the company can afford to give you. It would bring you back to work rested, happy to come back, and at ease with your new baby. (Or so you hope, seeing as how you have no idea yet what it will be like to be with a new baby.)

Now you have to make an appointment with the boss. This is the man who hasn't taken a day off in three years, and hates it when employees take more than a week of vacation at a time. Or this is the woman who fought so hard to become supervisor that she never stopped to start a family. Or this is the line supervisor who barely gives permission for bathroom breaks. How are you going to win this one?

You are going to focus, that's how. For the moment, stop thinking about that baby, the new nursery, the cute baby clothes, the little booties—or even the anxiety you may be feeling about how good a mom you're going to be. Keep the brown paper bag next to your bed, and breathe into it for panic attacks. You can't afford to let that anxiety distract you from your mission. Call a friend about your plans for the nursery later. Right now, realize that your boss doesn't care about any of those things.

What your boss cares about is how the work will get done.

So right now, that's what you have to care about, too, if you are going to get the time and money you need to afford those little hats and mittens and booties. Oh, and need I say, the mortgage and the car payments. What you need is a well-thought-out plan, a written proposal that will describe exactly how your work will get done while you're out.

Your boss also wants to know that this is a proposal worth reading. He wants to be reassured that you are REALLY coming back. It's a question in the back of everyone's mind—probably even yours, on some days. "The boss always panics that you won't come back from maternity leave," says my friend Daisy, who works for a brokerage firm. "Especially if you're his assistant."

So be prepared to open any negotiations about your leave with a positive attitude about your job, the company, and how happy you are with your situation. Even when you call to make an appointment to see him to present your proposal. If you expect him to take it seriously, he must believe, right from the start, that you are coming back. Otherwise, why bother to give you a leave at all?

"The key to a successful leave is to make sure your bosses know you want to come back," says Wendy, a lawyer in Southern California, who took two leaves of six and seven months. In both cases, she received full pay for the first three months. "So many attorneys didn't do that, and they didn't get good leaves." She suggests that you give your supervisor concrete evidence of your commitment by offering to come in for meetings, attend seminars, or anything else that go-getter workers in your office do. It might be as simple as keeping up with voice mail, e-mails, or faxes. Or just calling to keep in touch, and being available to answer questions that arise.

All these gestures show that you are willing to remain part of the give-and-take, and strengthen your boss's perception that you love your job, love your work, and love the company, and it's worth his time to do the right thing by you. Never mind that you're not certain about exactly what you want to do at this very moment. Stuff the ambivalence somewhere else. It's a natural reaction to the pressures you're feeling, but don't put it on display for your boss. Employers want to believe that you are a dedicated worker, and right now, you want to win them over.

Translated, that means: Act like a salesperson, even if you've never closed a sale in your life. You want to convince your boss that what you want is the same thing he wants. By the end of your negotiation, you want him to feel like he got a bargain, a great deal, like he's got a stellar employee here who could go anywhere she wanted, and he has done what he needs to do to keep her, that he negotiated shrewdly and won. To do that, you have to do what all good salespeople do: Think of the situation from his point of view. Anticipate his concerns and overcome his objections. Emphasize the benefits of giving you what you want and need. How will it boost the bottom line? What's in it for him?

And you must start by answering his most fundamental question: How the heck is your work going to get done while you're home with the new baby?

If we lived in a working world that valued women—all parents—more highly, you might reasonably expect company officials to help you answer that question. Given that over half the workforce is now female and most of us are in our childbearing years, you might think there would be some sort of systematic approach to handling maternity leave, especially if you work at a large company. Such as a budget for temporary workers. A pool of floaters. It could even be viewed as a great opportunity for the company: "Maternity leave can provide a chance for cross-training, grooming people for their next move, or just making sure that a company has someone trained to do most critical tasks when they lose someone," says Dana Friedman.

But we live in the real world and so hardly any companies actually use maternity leaves so creatively. Instead, they're likely to let the work pile up on your desk. Or pass it off to coworkers who will forever resent that "vacation" you took after you had the baby.

So you are the one who's going to have to answer your boss's question about how your work is going to get done. Sooner or later, your boss is going to put it to you, and you will have to find a solution. Julia, a pubic relations professional in Indianapolis, says, "I was told prior to my leaving that I had to find someone to cover my projects." She turned to interns, and told her supervisor and coworkers she'd be available by phone, and could even come in for an hour or two for a critical meeting. Happily, she never had to. But the fact she'd made the offer helped her get the leave she wanted.

It's to your advantage to do your own planning in advance, to figure out ways to stay in touch, and keep up on the gossip and company changes while you're out. This helps you maintain good relationships with everybody. After all, you don't want to be blindsided by news that your boss was fired or the company was sold while you were out on leave.

Thinking It Through

Here are some questions to ask yourself, questions that will help you think like your boss and come up with some good answers. Ask yourself the toughest questions you can think of, and get ready with some good solutions so he'll be ready to make you an offer you can't refuse:

Is there some work that only you can do because of your skills, knowledge, or contacts?

If so, think about whom you can cross-train, delegate work to, or groom in your office to keep up the work flow for at least the first month while you're away. Oftentimes, a younger and more junior person will welcome the opportunity to learn new skills or take on some new responsibilities for a while. Mary, director of the nursing staff at a small Catholic hospital, spent a fair amount of time teaching her staff key duties before she went out on leave. "By the time I left, they were well prepared to take over in a pinch. I was always available by phone, but I had mentored them enough that they hardly called me at all," she says. She took a full five months off.

What work is truly essential and must continue while you are away, and what work can wait?

This is a loaded question, of course, since we all like to think that *all* our work is essential—that we are indispensable. Even more to the point, even if we know that some of our work is not so essential, we're probably not keen on pointing that fact out to our supervisor. It doesn't take a genius to see that it's at least a little dangerous to say out loud that some of what we do can be suspended for a few weeks, much less a few months.

But thinking this way will help you set priorities for your temporary absence. You'll see the things that can wait and those that truly can't. And what you tell your boss is how you'll get those top priorities covered, and skip over the rest. You don't have to even bring up those duties. If he asks, have a plan for delegating them. Chances are, if they aren't too essential, he won't even think of them. When I took four months off from my magazine editing job, I took care of the priorities by assigning stories way ahead of deadlines, editing some key stories early, and delegating the mail and calls from publicity agents and other people pitching stories to my assistant. I gave her a list of the writers, agents, and publicists whom I knew I had to deal with personally, and let her handle the rest. The only work my editor-in-chief ever asked me about was the stories on a definite fast-track for the magazine, the ones that we knew were timely, competitive, or slated to get us widespread publicity. The stories that made her happy, the publisher happy.

Is it busy season? Are big projects underway?

If you work in retailing and your leave is going to happen right during the Christmas rush, or if you're an accountant and your leave is going to take place during tax season, your boss is going to be tempted to put all the pressure he can to get you back fast. Try to think of solutions that will keep the work on target and still give you time to enjoy your baby. My friend Barb, an accountant with one of the nation's big accounting firms, traded favors with other partners who were also moms, getting them to cover some of her key accounts while she was out on leave. "We all do our best to support each other, because we all want to be able to spend time with our families," she says. Happily, she managed to keep the work at bay during most of her three-month leave. "I had set up several partners to cover for me. Sometimes, they'd call and ask to schedule a conference call. I'd just laugh. They'd ask, 'When's a convenient time?' and I'd think, 'There is no convenient time.' I did do a couple of calls and a couple of meetings, but I don't really remember them," she says. E-mail proved to be a lifesaver, because it meant she could communicate with the office at odd hours, when the baby took a nap.

Clare, a friend of mine who works for Microsoft outside of Seattle, felt pretty relaxed with her first child. Both her managers were moms, and both encouraged her to take the five months she wanted. But the second time around, she had a huge project that had to be finished by the time she returned. She volunteered to do some work at home, to keep up with the office via her laptop, and to be available by phone and e-mail, as they needed her. "On that leave, it was important to stay in touch, to know the work was in good hands. And by keeping in touch, I was ready to fly back into it when I got back to work. It helped me readjust better."

If your company really can't spare you for the entire leave that you want, can you work out some other accommodation?

Linda, who works in a small retail store, wanted to hang on to her job, but she also understood that her boss couldn't afford to have her out of the store for the full two months she really wanted. There were only about fifteen people on the payroll in addition to members of the boss's family. So they worked out a temporary schedule that allowed her to return part-time for the second month, on a different shift. "I came in the evenings, and I was the one to close the store," she says. "That worked out well for me because my husband could get home to care for the baby, and I could show up at work on a shift that no one else liked."

If there's no one in your immediate office to help with your duties, can you bring in someone from another department? What about a temporary worker?

Cross-training someone else at the company can be sold as an advantage for your employer in the long run, since it means the firm will have someone to fill in for you when you're sick, on vacation, get promoted, or quit. The fact that you are still on staff and available to train that person before you go on leave is also an advantage to the firm. Many times, companies lose lots of time and money when someone goes out sick or suddenly quits because they don't have that time to plan and train a replacement.

Temporary workers from outside agencies can also fill in—and these days, it's possible to find temps to do almost any kind of job. There are accountants and even lawyers available for temporary stints; all you have to do is find the agencies that specialize in your line of work. Of course, your boss may understandably resist this solution. No one likes to bring in a stranger, especially when it's someone who will inevitably be gone in a few months. Shortsighted companies may also think they are going to save money while you're out. If the disability insurance company is paying your salary, they may be too stingy to lay out the money for a temp.

At least at first. The best way to sell this solution to your boss is to point out the costs of *not* hiring a warm body to get that work done. "We handle student applications, and I was going to be out during the busiest month of the application season, January," says Joanne. "When my boss acted a little queasy about bringing in someone new to handle that, I thought I was sunk. Then I reminded her of how the dean would feel if we were late processing the applications. The dean is her boss. And I volunteered to train the temp myself and be available by phone." Joanne got the temp hired, and even though there were a few mistakes along the way, things went relatively smoothly. And it was Joanne who absorbed the glitches, talking the temp through the work and talking with her coworkers when an application got routed to the wrong place. "I guess what I did was give my boss a stress-free maternity leave," she says with a laugh. "I had my bad days, but she didn't. And I got the time I needed."

Are you willing to do some work at home?

Don't be too quick to offer this solution. For most women, the time at home goes fast, and trying to squeeze in some work is simply a pipedream. Worse, worrying about getting work done in the early stages of your leave can create enormous, even unbearable, stress.

Thus, doing some work at home should be viewed as a last-resort solution. Still, it may be the only solution, the solution that gives you a break from going into the office and having to keep up a regular routine. You can even sleep a little later at home, after a bad night with the baby. So volunteering to work at home may simply be a survival technique to keep that paycheck coming. Taken in that light—rather than as part of a dreamy, flexible arrangement that will allow you to be home, cook gourmet meals, play with your baby, and also get work done—taken as a hard-nosed avenue toward paying the mortgage and keeping your job, it may work out.

"I had only been working at my company for about eighteen months when my son was born, " says Lynn. "I'd already taken a week's vacation for my honeymoon, so I didn't have much vacation time or sick leave built up. My employer does not provide paid maternity leave, so using vacation time, sick leave, short-term disability (only with doctor's approval and only after thirty days), or leave without pay were the only choices. Disability only pays about sixty percent of salary. So if you can't afford a pay cut (and who can with a new baby?), you have to come up with something else. I used up all my vacation and sick leave and then worked out an agreement to work at home and occasionally go in during my maternity leave. I don't recommend it unless it is a person's only choice, as it was in my case."

Once you've answered all these questions, and have a clear picture of how the work will be done while you're out, write up your proposal. Make it as concise as you can, while still covering all your bases. Start off with a few sentences that specify exactly how much time you want, what paid time you expect to use (vacation, personal days), and what unpaid time you believe is due to you.

Then dedicate the next few paragraphs to explaining how you believe the work can be covered while you're out. It's also a good idea to update your boss on the projects and duties you expect to complete before you go out.

Talking to the Boss

Now you're ready to make an appointment and meet with your supervisor. Request the meeting, and tell him you have a written proposal that lays everything out. Give it to him ahead of the meeting. Then, psych yourself up for this to be a positive encounter. If you feel intimidated, try to take it on as a project, like bringing along the illiterate or dealing with an anxious child. If this is a guy who's never changed a diaper and never wants to, if his wife is at home and he believes all wives should be home, handle him with kid gloves! Be respectful, professional, and patient. Don't get too friendly, and don't burden him with unnecessary details. Just be positive, upbeat, and to the point.

Above all, recognize that this is just one meeting to him, just one of his concerns, even though it is terribly important to you. What he wants from you are the answers, the winning arguments so he can feel confident that all will go smoothly—so *he* can win over *his* boss and give you what you want.

And don't expect him to put a lot of weight on that written proposal. Don't even expect him to have read it carefully—or even to have read it at all—when you meet with him. What he wants from you is the quick summary, the cheerleading session, the answers so he can move on to the mechanics—notifying human resources, the insurance company, and other company officials—without a problem.

In the best of all possible worlds, you'll be sitting down with a supportive boss, who wants to make sure you get the time off you need and return rested and ready to work. A publicist who works for a giant public relations firm was worried about asking for as much time as she wanted. But her boss was a working mom who pushed her to ask for even more. "She advised me to truly enjoy my leave and the experience of motherhood, to not concern myself with work because I'd never get that time again. She gave me the comfort and security I needed to go into my leave and my new role as mother without the added worry of what was going on back at the office—to my job, my accounts, my career, and I thank her for that."

But if you run into resistance, don't give up. Another friend at a small agency had to go back to the principals of the agency (all men) repeatedly before she got what she wanted: a three-month leave with a three-day work week when the leave was over. "It was a small agency, with less than fifteen employees, so they weren't covered by any laws," she recalls. "I was the first employee to ask for a maternity leave. I started writing e-mail to them about the need to discuss my leave when I was three months pregnant, but they didn't respond. They didn't respond until I was six months along!"

Apparently, they were consulting with lawyers because they were uncertain about just what kind of maternity leave policy they wanted to establish. Finally, at the six-month point, they sat down and met. "To my chagrin, nothing was decided even then!" she says. "I was going crazy, because I needed to make plans." The sticking point, not surprisingly, was her gradual reentry to work. "They were far more concerned with the idea that I'd switch to a part-time schedule than with giving me the twelve weeks off that I wanted."

Over those months of negotiating, she wrote memos to justify her request, gathering facts and figures and even documenting what other ad agencies were doing. "I began to call it my treatise on maternity leave," she laughs. Still, nothing was settled until she was out on leave. "I was completely exhausted by the negotiations and I'd gone out on leave feeling so unsettled. But I just decided to forget about it, take the leave, and see what happened."

In the end, her persistence and her arguments apparently won her bosses over. "When I called my boss to discuss the day I was coming back, he just said, 'Which three days do you want to come in?' " she says. "I guess all that lobbying paid off. I just tell other women not to get angry, not to give up, to just keep selling your case."

Cover All Your Bases

Once you have an agreement, confirm it in writing with your boss and the human resources department, or anyone else who may need to sign off on the deal. Having it all on paper is a simple and easy protection for you, a clear understanding of the terms of the deal. In most cases, you can then stuff it in a file and forget about it. But you'll be mighty glad you have that document if anything changes at work while you're out. It will be the proof of your agreement if your boss gets promoted, quits, or switches jobs while you're out on leave—or if you run into a dispute about the time that you have been granted.

By law, you must also be sure to follow certain steps as you go out on leave. The federal Family and Medical Leave Act specifies that you give at least thirty days' notice of your intention to take the leave, unless you have to go out quickly because of a medical emergency. You may also need to have a note from your doctor certifying your condition. That medical note may be particularly critical if you are going to be collecting disability paychecks while you're out. The disability insurance company will want documentation of your medical condition, and may even have its own nurse keep in touch with you while you're out.

One Last Word

Given the nature of different bosses, different companies, and even of different women with their own temperaments and talents, there's no doubt that negotiating a maternity leave will be a different experience for each and every one of us. But my friend Bonnie told me one thing that I have never forgotten, and I pass along the thought to all moms in the workplace, not only for this negotiation, but also for all the other negotiations you'll be doing now that you have a demanding life outside of work. "Never show your weak side," Bonnie said to me. In other words, go into the negotiation believing that if you don't get what you want and need, you can walk away and they will be the losers. In her case, she got exactly the leave she wanted, in part because she never let down her guard. "They were very accommodating about maternity leave because they wanted to ensure I'd come back. No one else can do the things I know how to do. So they let me work at home whenever I needed to, and let me take a little longer than official policy allows," says Bonnie. "Financially I can't afford to quit. But I'd never tell them that. It would make me vulnerable."

WHEN THERE'S A PROBLEM

Okay. I know. You've heard about those so-called family-friendly companies. But you haven't ever met anyone who works for one.

Even if you know someone who works for one, she tells you the publicity is a lie. Good policies exist on paper, but hardly anyone gets those benefits.

Anyway, you know your own boss. He's an old-fashioned kind of guy. Well, he's a Neanderthal. He's convinced all moms belong at home. His own wife quit working when they had kids, and he's even told you that's the best thing for children. And most of the women who've worked for him quit when they had babies.

He'll be the first to tell you it's because they wanted to be home. But you know it's because he's a rather difficult boss to start with, and he gets worse when he learns a woman is pregnant.

How can you be sure that your rights are protected?

Start out by knowing exactly what laws cover you, what the company policies are and the sorts of leaves your company has granted in the past. For a quick and accurate look at the legal issues, visit the National Partnership on Women and Families Web site at www.nationalpartnership.org. There, you'll find an overview of your legal rights. You can also call the National Association of Working Women's free job hotline, to get a rundown on your rights (1-800-522-0925).

After you know what's what, approach your boss in a confident, professional, and cooperative tone, laying out the time you need, as if you expect him to grant your request without question.

If you run into a problem, keep notes on all your conversations and any interactions that worry you. Call Nine-to-Five or a local women's rights organization to find an employment law attorney who can give you sound advice. Don't be too quick to think legal action might solve your problems, however. Pregnancy discrimination is incredibly difficult to prove and the legal process is demanding, slow, and outrageously expensive.

It is preferable to educate yourself about your rights and take your case to the human resources department, your union rep, or any senior manager who might be willing to intervene. Let that person know that you are having some trouble getting the time off you are entitled to, and that you'd like to get some help negotiating the situation. You may even want to pursue a transfer to another department.

If problems persist, you may have no recourse other than legal action or quitting. Bringing in an attorney to negotiate on your behalf will most certainly sour things with your boss—but at that point, it may no longer matter. And your courage to face such discrimination down may make the workplace better for other new moms in the future!

YOU'RE PREGNANT—CAN YOU BE FIRED?

By now, it's no novelty for an employer to have a pregnant worker on the job. And most know it's against the law to treat you differently if you are pregnant.

You cannot be fired, refused a new job, demoted, or transferred to a lesser position if you work at a firm with fifteen or more employees.

Well, that's the law.

And we all know there are some bosses who insist on doing things their way. Ways that violate the law.

"I actually had a man tell me, 'You realize no one will hire you while you're pregnant,'" says Carol, a management consultant who was job-hunting during her second pregnancy. Other women tell me they've suddenly been shut out of key meetings, given lesser assignments, or told their job will change when they return to work.

If such things start to happen to you, keep track of them. Don't think—or threaten—legal action right away. Discrimination cases are hard to prove and even harder to win. Worse, your child might be a teenager by the time you get any satisfaction.

Still, most companies don't want to risk trouble. So if your boss starts to treat you differently, keep a log. And remind him that you're still interested in and capable of doing everything you did before. If he persists, let him know that you believe he's treating you differently because of the pregnancy and you also know that such treatment is illegal. Often, that turns the situation around.

If it doesn't, you can apply for a transfer to another department and a more compatible boss—or you can take your case to the human resources department or even to an outside attorney.

For advice and coaching on how to handle such a case, call the toll-free Job Problem Hotline (800-522-0925) run by 9 to 5, the National Association of Working Women. Or contact a local attorney specializing in employment law.

YOU'RE ON LEAVE—CAN YOU BE LAID OFF?

The story is not so unusual, and may become more so if the economy becomes troubled. You're on maternity leave, and suddenly you get a call. It happened to Mary during her fifth week out on leave. "My boss called to tell me that due to company reorganizations there would not be a position for me to return to," she says.

"Reorganization is a common excuse used by employers. Or restructuring," says Judith Vladeck, one of the nation's leading employment discrimination attorneys. And when that's the storyline from your boss, it's hard to prove the company is discriminating against you—unless the only people "reorganized" out of a job are pregnant or on family leave.

Usually things aren't that straightforward. To get the lowdown on just what rights you have when you're on leave, visit the Web site of the National Partnership for Women and Families at www.nationalpartnership.org. At this site you'll find answers to the most commonly asked questions about federal and state family leave laws, as well as details on your rights when you're pregnant or out on leave.

Chapter 4

Breast or Bottle?
The First Hurdle

When the lactation nurse walked into my hospital room, I knew I was in trouble. "Oh, my God!" was all she said when she looked at my breasts. Then, "Don't they hurt?"

Hurt? Nothing hurt. I'd been on Percodan (a painkiller) for a few days, in the wake of a cesarean section. Nothing hurts when you're on that drug. I was giddy with the excitement of Rachel's birth, smiling like a maniac. Look at this baby! I wanted to shout. Just look at her! A few hours ago she was inside me. Now, she's out! A miracle.

No, my breasts did not hurt.

But when I looked down, I could see why the nurse had reacted the way she did. My usually small breasts were nearly the size of, well, watermelons. And they were hard. Hard as very green watermelons. I was engorged.

I vaguely remembered reading about this. Also, that I shouldn't let this happen. But there I was, with breasts from hell. Or at least, without the Percodan, they would have been.

I spent the next three days learning how to get them down to normal size, with the help of hot showers—which I began to take about every fifteen minutes, or so it seemed—and of getting Rachel to nurse as frequently as possible.

Once the engorgement was over, I was introduced to a new sort of discomfort: sore nipples. Many salves and gentle massages later, Rachel and I had the hang of nursing. And I loved it.

Our success was due largely to the help I got, right in the hospital, from a lactation consultant who worked on the maternity ward. She's the one who introduced me to the salves and massages, and urged me to keep Rachel right next to me as much as I could. That meant that Rae would nurse on demand, and keep me from getting engorged again. It meant my milk supply would grow to meet her demand. And it meant that we'd establish our own techniques and rhythms. I did truly come to understand why everyone says nursing is the most natural thing in the world. It is so physical. I really did "let down" when Rachel cried, the milk ready to flow, sometimes even leaking after it fully came in.

But breastfeeding can also be one of the most trying parts of new motherhood. And these days, most women are rushed home after delivery and there is no one around to help. "My milk coming in was more painful than delivery, I swear! No one warned me about that," recalls one new mom. She gave up within nine days. But she didn't want to, and my bet is that she wouldn't have if only she'd had a little help and encouragement.

Going back to work complicates the process, of course. Many of us hardly get the milk supply established in the first six weeks, and far too many of us have to rush back to our jobs by then.

That's why I devote this chapter to the trials of juggling breastfeeding and work. It's the first hurdle you face after birth, it's demanding, and it won't take you long to find out for yourself that everyone has an opinion and some free advice on the topic. It seems there's just nothing like breastfeeding to light everyone up and get them yakking at you. Everybody from your mother-in-law to your coworkers have some little nugget of advice. Some of it is useful. For example, one of my neighbors passed on to me a tip to run a hair dryer next to her colicky son to calm him down, so she could successfully nurse. "It was the noise," she recalls. "Somehow, he'd just quiet right down, and then I could pick him up." You don't learn tricks like that from books on breastfeeding.

But just as often, you'll find their opinions have more to do with them than with you. And hardly any of it has to do with the practical stuff. Instead, they'll tell you what they think of nursing or bottles, how they feel about breastfeeding in public, how modest or immodest you are, and whether it's pleasant to have such a close physical relationship with your child. Even whether it's "right" or "wrong" to breastfeed. These are hot-button issues in America today, even sparking legal debates about whether breastfeeding should be allowed in public and whether employers should be required to support you if that's the route you take.

And then there's the medical community. With doctors and major health organizations backing breastfeeding's benefits, your pediatrician may act like you have no other choice.

I nursed both my kids until they were about a year old. When I was at work I used an electric pump to express milk from my breasts, saved it in a cool pack, and took it home so that it could be given to the baby throughout the next day at home. I gradually tapered off nursing until I no longer needed to pump at all at work, and just nursed when I was home. I had plenty of rough spots along the way. Those breasts from hell with Rachel got a little worse before they got better, especially after I stopped taking the painkillers. With Dan, it was hard early on when we were separated for a few days: Like many newborns, he suffered a mild case of jaundice and had to be readmitted to the hospital. Not a serious health problem, not even a serious situation for a mentally balanced person. But as a new mother with raging hormones, I went nuts for a few days, as my milk was coming in and I could not be near my baby. I was certain we'd never succeed at nursing.

But we did. Within a few days, we were so readjusted and on target that he didn't ever take a bottle. (The next hurdle for this working mom.)

I'm glad that I nursed both my babies. But I also believe that moms today need latitude and support when it comes to the Bottle or Breast Question. Especially those who will have relatively short maternity leaves. My ability to carry on had to do with many things, including having privacy at work and the sort of job where no one policed my hours or told me when I could go on break. I could just shut my office door when I had to express my milk. I also had an incredibly supportive work environment.

I have talked to friends who've managed to keep on nursing their babies even under the most difficult circumstances. They've expressed milk in the ladies' room at work, even in the toilet stalls, because it was literally the only place and time they had to get it done. They also learned how to use manual pumps or even express milk with no pump at all—something that earns a woman the Nobel Prize for Motherhood in my book. These friends were totally devoted to breastfeeding, even when work separated them from their infants.

I say more power to them, but let's give the rest of our friends a break. I think many new moms need to know it really is okay to use a bottle if that's what works, or if it's simply their preference. I've seen some women so worn down and exhausted as they tried to breastfeed and work that they didn't even enjoy their new babies. At times, their dogged determination to breastfeed no matter what has even put them at serious risk. A few years back, the *Wall Street Journal* documented several dozen cases of babies who got dehydrated and had to be hospitalized because some moms felt compelled to nurse, even when their milk supply was inadequate to give babies enough nutrition. These women felt enormous guilt at the idea of using a bottle, so they kept on trying to breastfeed, until the situation grew so dire for both them and their babies that they wound up in the emergency rooms at local hospitals. That's extreme, of course, but indicative of the pressures many women feel today to nurse no matter what.

For their sake, I say, let's ease up a bit. My own mother bottlefed all five of us, and everyone is healthy today. My mom never quite understood why I liked nursing my own children so much. My mother's experience with breastfeeding was something akin to that of my friend Laurie, who quit nursing a few weeks into her maternity leave. The process never went smoothly, she didn't like it, and her son was fussy. "The best moment of my first maternity leave was the moment I gave up breastfeeding. I finally started to enjoy my baby. He was also less fussy and hungry all the time."

There are even many unsung benefits to bottlefeeding your baby. Like, Dad or big brother or big sister gets to join in and bond with the new baby. Like, no pumping, no breast pads to protect your blouses, no embarrassing moments when your milk lets down while you are on the job or in some other public place.

So this chapter is devoted to giving you some strategies to make it through this first big hurdle as a working mom. Instead of opinions, I'll offer up the strategies my friends and I have found to make breastfeeding work, for a short or a long while, to blend breast and bottle, and to make everything work with working.

Right from the Start: Tactics at the Hospital

You may wind up, as I did, in a hospital so supportive of breastfeeding that they have a lactation consultant right on staff who visits all the new moms. It's certainly getting to be more common.

Then again, you may not. After the birth of my second child, the nurses hardly even showed up. Daniel was born on July 3, right before the big national holiday, the staff was short-handed, and a whole new team of interns and residents had just rotated into the ward. They had no one to talk to me about breastfeeding. In fact, they had no one to talk to me much at all. They had a teen mom suffering from an infection, and an asthmatic mom who'd had an emergency during delivery. I was hardly their priority. In fact, there were times I wasn't even sure they remembered we were there. If I hadn't known what to do, I'd have been in trouble.

And not just about nursing technique. Even in these days when medical organizations pay enormous lip service to the value of breastfeeding, I learned that you have to be your own advocate in the hospital. You must insist that the baby be left with you as much as possible at first, even if it's easier for the doctors to return her to the nursery. You must also insist that a sign is posted on her bassinet in the nursery that no formula be given, and no sugar water, either, until she has nursed.

Otherwise, you're left to the whims of the particular nurses on duty, their feelings about breastfeeding, and their habits while on duty. One friend of mine learned the hard way just how difficult that can be. She'd had trouble getting her newborn to stay at the breast the first few days after birth. She'd already had two other children, so she found this odd. The mystery was solved as she was checking out. She then learned the nurses had been bottlefeeding her daughter all along. "I think it was an excuse to hold her. All the nurses in labor and delivery loved the babies, and loved holding and feeding them. So they were bringing her to me with a full tummy, but no one had bothered to tell me this until we were leaving the hospital. I guess I should have been more forceful about my wishes to breastfeed!" she says.

The second thing you need to do is find help when you need it. Everyone tells you how natural breastfeeding is, but there are so many little things to learn along the way, like how to relax, calm the baby, and get him to latch on to the breast if he's fussy at first. If there's no lactation consultant, try to lasso a friendly nurse or even a nurse's aid to help you learn these things. Some babies aren't strong on sucking; others like to suck all the time, but can't settle down at first. One friend learned to offer her newborn a pacifier before the breast, to get her focused and settled down.

Someone knowledgeable can also tell you what's normal and what's not. No one told my friend Maria about engorgement, and she hadn't read up on it, the way I had. She wasn't on Percodan or any other painkiller when her milk came in, she didn't get her baby to the breast right away, and she wasn't prepared for what followed. "No one told me what it's like when your milk comes in. My breasts were so large and tender. I remember it vividly, and it was a little scary, until a nurse showed me how to get the baby to latch on to my breast and relieve the pressure."

If you are in the hospital for a few days and find some especially helpful people, you might even get a head start on learning how to express milk, while you still have someone to consult. It's a skill you'll inevitably need to develop for your return to work, and like everything else you confront as a new parent, you're likely to find yourself utterly clueless at first. Some hospitals may have an electric pump you can use, or know a nearby pharmacy that will rent one on a short-term basis, even for a week at a time, for you to try out and take home. Nurses and lactation consultants can also recommend those salves for sore breasts and show you other ways to get comfortable. Minor breast infections are not uncommon in new moms, and the nurses can also teach you how to spot the signs of an infection, or head one off, usually simply by nursing your baby a little more often.

If you leave the hospital in a hurry, as so many women must, enlist a friend or relative to help with breastfeeding when you get home. If you don't have anyone nearby, but do have a computer, there is some good help online. Lots of moms and experts can be found at www.breastfeeding.com, every hour of the day and night, with lots of tips for everything from expressing milk to relaxation techniques to help your milk let down. These days, you can even hire a lactation consultant to come to your home and give you a few tips to smooth things out.

La Leche League, a longstanding international group dedicated to the promotion of breastfeeding, offers support groups, advice, and brochures to women. It has chapters in most cities. Your local La Leche League chapter, listed in your phone book, can refer you to consultants who are board-certified, that is, people who've actually taken courses and been officially approved to teach new moms about the art of breastfeeding. One caveat, however: Make sure that anyone you contact through La Leche League supports your need and desire to work after the baby is born. Some of the most ardent breastfeeding advocates, including many in La Leche League chapters, argue that all moms should quit work and be home with their new babies. With everything else you have to cope with at this stage, you don't need that kind of guilt trip. Many experts, friends, and coworkers will be supportive and give you the advice you need. Avoid the ones who aren't!

Plotting Your Return to the Job

As you try to master the fundamentals of breastfeeding, you may panic about work. How in the world can you combine breastfeeding and a job? Some days, you may even wonder how you can combine breastfeeding and *anything* else. "I think I was nursing sixteen hours a day at first. That was absolutely the only thing that the baby wanted to do," says Joyce. "I never imagined that I'd be able to leave the house, let alone go back to work, in those first days. I was totally freaked out." Of course, things changed in that first month. "After the first few weeks, there was still a lot of chaos, but we began to establish a rhythm. I could see it was going to be okay."

So it goes for most of us. If you can be a little Zen about these early days and accept the chaos, you'll find things do settle down. Nearly everyone I know noticed a change at three weeks, and certainly by the classic six-week marker that doctors call the recovery period. By then, most had fallen into a regular routine with their babies, nursing three or four times during the day or even less.

And that's when you can start to focus on the logistics of getting back to work, and all that free advice people are giving you or that you've read in magazines. You may already have heard some of the usual tips: Make sure you offer the baby a bottle at least once a day, so she'll get used to it. Be sure that you start expressing milk right away, so that you get the hang of it. Have your husband or a caregiver offer the baby a bottle at night. Don't offer formula at all.

Some of it will be contradictory and confusing. For instance, many people will tell you: Offer a bottle right away so your baby gets used to it or you may have trouble getting him to take a bottle when you return to work. Then others will warn you to never, ever offer your baby a bottle in the early days or she may refuse your breast.

You hear these different things because both are true—for different babies and different moms. My first child would take a bottle or the breast, no problem. That got me so relaxed that I didn't worry about how things would go with my second. But I should have. He steadfastly refused a bottle. We survived my return to work only through the good graces of a caregiver who taught him to take formula from a spoon and then a drinking cup.

The consensus among most experts is that it *is* a good idea to start introducing a bottle and learning how to pump about two weeks before you are going back to work, if not sooner. At this point, it's also a good idea to start pumping even more than you'll need to, just to build up your milk supply for the transition. Try to pump right after you feed the baby at least once or twice a day. This will help you get used to pumping and give you a little extra milk to stash in the freezer when you first start out. It's insurance against the stress lots of us feel at the beginning. Most of us find it hard to relax and let down with a pump the way we do with our babies, and we may be anxious about getting back to work. So our milk supplies may wane a little. Taking this step to express a little extra a little more often while you're still at home with the baby is a little insurance plan. You'll have the extra milk, and the extra experience pumping.

And any extra experience with pumping is a very good thing. Take it from me. So is a sense of humor. No one tells you when you get pregnant that you are going to be pumping your breasts in nine or ten months. Amy described her first reaction to pumping milk from her breasts: "I wanted to do this for my baby, but it just felt unnatural at first. Just weird to hook up my breasts to a pump. I felt like a cow! I didn't like it at first. It took me three days, experimenting with three different pumps before I got anything at all. I was beginning to think it was impossible! And then it happened! I let down and saw that milk spurt out! Then I knew it was going to be okay!"

GIVE THAT BABY A BOTTLE!

I had the nightmare experience of my second child refusing a bottle when I went back to work. He wasn't yet on solid foods, and I was saved only by the fact that my very dedicated caregiver managed to get him to suck formula off a spoon. From the e-mail I receive, I see that many women have this problem. "My husband watched Jenny in the mornings, and brought her to my office so she could nurse. She was very stubborn and would not take a bottle under any circumstances," says Erica, a paralegal. "Thank god she learned to drink from a bottle at six months!"

Rather than find yourself in this position, try to give your baby at least one bottle a day, after the third week or so, to prepare her for the days when you are back on the job.

Two Magic Words: Electric Pump

Like many of us, Amy managed to express her first milk with a manual pump, one of those plastic or glass jobs that looks like a part of a childhood chemistry set. To succeed, you must maneuver the thing until you have exactly the right position and the right motion to create the suction your baby does, to get the milk to let down and flow. For most of us the process is awkward, unwieldy, and unnerving, especially when combined with all the other tasks we must learn as new moms.

Many women soldier on with manual pumps—until they discover hospital-grade electric pumps, an appliance I believe no working mom should be without. "With my daughter, I used a hand pump in the ladies'-room stall. How I did that, I don't know! I nursed until she was fifteen months," says Lucy. "With our son, I rented a dual (meaning you can express milk from both breasts at once) industrial electric pump; what a huge difference. This machine, albeit large, and I were inseparable."

You can rent or buy these pumps from a local pharmacy and leave them at work, if you have somewhere secure to store them. The best ones, "hospital-grade" pumps, are heavy and big, and run to about $200 to buy, but most pharmacies that carry them will rent them. The most popular breast pump manufacturers, Medela and Ameda Egnell, make more than one model of machine, including battery-operated ones that are lighter and more portable. By experimenting, you'll figure out what works best for you. Most women swear by the strongest ones, which get the job done in as little as five or ten minutes, relieving any engorgement you may experience and giving you several ounces of breast milk to take home to your baby.

These days, it's also possible to find used electric breast pumps for sale, through friends or even over the Internet. Taking this route can save you money, but health officials warn that you must make your choice carefully. Some pumps aren't meant to be used by more than one person because they have parts that can't be completely cleaned, and many medical experts believe that certain viruses, including AIDS and at least one type of leukemia, may be transmitted through human breast milk. Because of this, the Food and Drug Administration now requires that some breast pumps be labeled "single patient" or "single user" to indicate that they should never be shared. The most powerful ones, the ones most people call "hospital grade," have removable parts that can be sterilized and used over and over again by different moms. That's why they can be rented.

Back at Work: A Place and Time of Your Own

Once you're back on the job, you'll probably need to express milk at least once a day, if not more, at least for a while. Lucky you, if you have a private office and can just shut the door. You may even work for one of those amazing companies that now has a "lactation room" with company-owned breast pumps, refrigerators, a sink, and a comfortable, quiet, and private place to sit.

Those amenities allow you to do everything right: take your time, relax, store your milk, and even wash your hands afterward. The milk you express will last for up to eight days in the refrigerator and even longer if you freeze it. Happily, these days you can find all the equipment and accessories you need—for example, plastic bags for storage—at the pharmacy where you purchase your pump.

But most women in the United States don't work in an office where there is a lactation room—or even much privacy for expressing milk. They simply make the best of a bad situation, learning to pump in the ladies' room, over the sink, at lunch, or during coffee breaks. Or they commandeer someone else's office, a conference room where they can lock the door, or any other room that offers some privacy and quiet. Often lacking a refrigerator to store the milk in, they tote cold packs to and from work along with their pumps. Though these circumstances are far from ideal, many women make it work and even enjoy the experience.

Elizabeth really did succeed, thanks in large part to the way folks treated her on the job. "It was a totally positive experience. Thanks to an electrical outlet in the ladies' room, I could hook up my pump and take breaks and keep on going. You would not believe the number of positive things the other women would say when they came in and saw me pumping away."

Donna found she could get away with one pumping session at lunch. But some women, especially those with private offices and jobs that offer some autonomy, say they pump twice a day if they can, at least for the first month or two back at work.

Many also find that over time, the need to pump milk lessens. As babies begin to take solid food they nurse less, and once your milk supply is established, you may be able to nurse your baby on an "as-needed" basis when you are home and skip the pumping altogether. That's what happened to me with my second child. I cut out the pumping when he was about seven months old, and my milk supply was not compromised. Donna had a similar experience, starting even sooner. "I never pumped milk after I went back to work at twelve weeks. My daughter took formula during the day, and

I still nursed her in the morning, after work, and before bed until she was nine months old. My milk adjusted to her schedule," she says.

The main thing to remember is that breastfeeding is really a dance you and your baby do, a relationship that you invent together, one following the other's cues. There are no right or wrong techniques, just the ones that work for you. Try all the strategies that people suggest, and eventually, you and your child will cobble together the strategies that work for you. When you run into a problem, be creative, like Beth, who wanted to introduce formula and avoid the need to pump much after she returned to work. "I nursed my daughter full-time for eight weeks. Then we tried to introduce a bottle with formula. She refused it, so then we mixed formula with breast milk, and she took the bottle just fine. I gradually reduced the percentage of breast milk to formula, so by the time I went back to work, she would take formula during the day," she says.

When You Must Travel

A growing number of women must travel on business, an event that used to fill me with guilt like no other. Like many other women I know, I simply refused to travel at all until my first child was three. But, also like many women I know, I've come to learn that it was I who suffered, not my children. Babies can be very flexible, especially when left in familiar surroundings with Dad and a trusted caregiver. The first time I came home after a night away, my daughter and her father laughed as they showed me all the wonderful things they'd done while I was away. Playing records, singing, eating ice cream. Going to bed late, of course. Other women I know had similar unfounded angst, especially when they thought it would interrupt or ruin their breast-feeding regimen.

"My worst moment as a working mom was when my daughter was four months old, and I had to make an overnight trip to Atlanta," says Mary, a sales rep who lives in Florida. "I had missed my flight, I was totally stressed out, and then I realized I'd forgotten my breast pump. I was a complete wreck, and sure that I'd ruined my milk supply."

She did leak all over her pajamas and right through a couple of breast pads the next day. But on her return home, she and her daughter got right back into the rhythm. "It was a lesson for me, that Dad and daughter did fine without me—I was the only one that was a wreck."

She now advises other moms to forget the angst, but not the pump. You need to be able to express milk, so you can stay comfortable and keep up your milk supply in those early months. She also suggests building in extra time, extra treats, and preparation for the inevitable distraction and pain of missing your baby, so you can function at a normal level. "I'm sure I missed that flight because I was so upset about having to leave my daughter. I've learned to just take it slow and even to enjoy those occasional nights away. They can even be luxurious," she says. "as long as you don't forget that pump!"

Some executive and professional moms now get permission to bring their babies and caregivers along to conventions or meetings that last more than one night, although, needless to say, that kind of arrangement is still rare.

Weaning

Before I had my babies, I assumed that weaning them would be difficult for both of us. But both my children weaned themselves, as they grew into the world. For Rachel, it happened when she was only seven months. By then, any slight distraction—someone talking, the dog barking—would interrupt her nursing. She was also eager to get walking, and started that at eight months. Maybe she just wanted her independence. Whatever the reason, she stopped nursing gradually, cutting out feedings, and I finally just gave up.

Dan went much the same way, only not until he was about fourteen months old. And in the meantime, he went through periods where nursing was clearly a source of comfort more than nourishment. On some weekends he'd want to nurse almost like a newborn, every few hours. Then, when he was ready, he just stopped.

As with everything else in breastfeeding, you can learn some techniques that can speed the process and make it easier, like making yourself less available when you're home, or having your spouse do the feedings from a bottle. Books on breastfeeding and weaning are full of useful tips, as are the Web sites like www.breastfeeding.com. The longer your child continues to nurse, the more difficult the weaning may be. Toddlers can be extremely insistent about wanting to continue and I know moms who find it embarrassing to weather tantrums about it in public.

But with some insistence on your part, nature does take its course. Kids do grow more independent, and move on. And for most women, the weaning process is ever so much easier than getting started. Although, the end of nursing may also make you downright sad, an unmistakable sign that you no longer have a real baby, but a growing, strapping toddler!

What the Experts Don't Tell You

After talking with many other women, I've decided that there are a few other facts every mom needs to know about combining breastfeeding and a job. Knowing these things can make a huge difference in your expectations, your plans, and your ultimate adjustment. They are things that you can't necessarily control or change, but you can adapt and accept, which makes for smoother sailing.

Babies Are All So Different

First of all, perfectly normal babies are so perfectly different that it can drive you insane. I would read the books and talk to friends and try to assure myself that Rachel was getting enough breast milk and gaining the right amount of weight. But it wasn't easy. Unlike all the reports of half-hour nursing sessions and even daylong marathon sessions, Rachel was never interested in nursing for very long. In fact, she nursed for five minutes on each breast and that was it, right from the start. And only once every four hours, at the most.

At a year, she weighed exactly fifteen pounds—a veritable lightweight. Luckily, my pediatrician was relaxed, noting that she was never sick, nor was she fussy. He assured me that he thought everything was fine . . . but. But, he said, he wanted to check her out. Her weight could indicate a medical condition known as "failure to thrive."

Of course, I was worried sick when he ordered a few tests. I wondered whether breastfeeding had been a mistake. But all the tests came back fine, and to this day, she's been an extremely robust child. About a year later, Evey, one of her great-aunts, told me that all her children had been exactly the same. What a relief to hear!

Rachel's appetite was so slight, however, that every time I tried to express milk I was lucky to get even an ounce, let alone the two to four that the books say is necessary. I tried every kind of pump, slaving away, but could never produce those magical four ounces. So it worried me, until that wonderful great-aunt calmed me down.

Meanwhile, every other new mom I knew did nothing but nurse! Claudia, the mom I talked to most, never even got dressed in the first month because her daughter wanted to do nothing but breastfeed. And when she pumped, she got four to six ounces at a time. She was always stashing milk in her freezer. Of course, she worried that her baby was gaining *too much*.

We both adjusted to nursing and working. Both our daughters turned out fine, neither underweight nor overweight.

Timing Is Everything

The timing of your return to work will dramatically affect everything about the way you juggle breastfeeding and your job. If you have to go back at six or eight weeks, it's going to be radically different than if you return at three or four months.

At six or eight weeks, you and your baby may still be establishing your routines, and a regular milk supply. There may still be days when your baby's going through growth spurts and suddenly demands to nurse every other hour, which builds up your supply. And she may still be waking once or twice a night. So unless you're an Olympic athlete, you're going to be as tired as all get out. If you add colic to this mix, a condition that, if present, usually doesn't ease up until about six weeks, you simply have a whole different set of challenges than other moms. Your baby may be crying incessantly, making nursing seem impossible.

That doesn't mean you won't succeed. But for the moment, it's better to concede that your life will often feel like a four-alarm fire and you need different strategies than other moms. For example, you may not be able to focus on pumping and giving the baby a bottle two weeks before your return to work. Don't worry about it. Just do the best you can. Try to maintain a sense of humor, and know that life will slow down and have less of a hurry-up, last-minute, chaotic quality in the months that follow. And you and your baby may end up being more flexible in the long run.

In fact, if you are reading this book and it is the middle of the night, and you are looking for some answers about how you can get up and go to work tomorrow, just put this book down. Walk over to the family computer, if you have one, and visit www. breastfeeding.com and find other moms to chat with who've been through it. What you need more than anything is affirmation, and other moms are often the first to offer the support you need—to tell you that you are not too crazy, too tired, or too lazy to go on.

Or maybe that you *are* too tired and crazy, and need to call in sick tomorrow and get some sleep, so that you can continue to go on.

If you don't have a computer, go to sleep. Right now. What you really need is rest.

If your mood persists, try to find another solution, such as a reduced schedule at work for a while. Even working at home for a day a week can help ease the pressure until you and your baby are more settled. Or working a six-hour day for a while. If you are covered by the Family and Medical Leave Act, remember that you can take your maternity leave in increments—half-days, part-time work, or even quarter-days, if your employer agrees. You might stretch the last month of leave to two months of half-time. That way, you can get a little more rest, recover, and be a better mom and a better worker for your company.

Support on the Job

Finally, your ability to continue breastfeeding after you return to work will be hugely affected by the support—or lack of it—you get on the job, and the kind of job you have. Without breaks to express milk, without privacy and a place to store the milk you express, you're not nearly as likely to succeed. Even having something as simple as an electrical outlet in the right spot for your breast pump can make a difference!

Brenda succeeded largely because of the atmosphere at work. In fact, expressing milk at work made her life feel all of a piece, creating a time at work when she could pause and think about her newborn. "Breastfeeding was a way for me to stay connected to my baby after returning to work. I could break from my job for a few minutes during the day to just stop and think about and do for my baby. I could also chat with other nursing mothers and trade stories and advice— something all new mothers long to do, even when they're wearing a suit!" she says. She even got some work done, on occasion. "I would often catch up on my in box while I pumped," she says.

For another friend, the logistics were just too daunting. A public relations specialist, she had to commute from New Jersey to New York City every day, an hour each way. "I wanted to breastfeed, but with commuting, traveling, etc. it just became a nightmare. I remember being called into a meeting one time before I could pump and I began to lactate. I panicked. It was so difficult to get up and walk out unobtrusively during a major meeting. I put my jacket on and hoped I would make it through the meeting. I did, but when I got back to my office, my blouse was soaked. I decided then and there to give it up."

For others, there is outright hostility. "My coworkers resented my taking pumping breaks, so I did it less and less. This made me miserably uncomfortable, since my breasts got sore," says one. "But it was easier than dealing with their remarks." Not surprisingly, she gave up on nursing within weeks of her return to work.

Studies show just how important such attitudes are. You are only about half as likely to continue nursing if you lack support on the job.

You can try to change those attitudes, however, just as you can bargain for a longer, more flexible maternity leave. Indeed, companies that do provide lactation rooms often started the practice only after a number of moms came to them and asked for help. Smart employers are beginning to see that such support can save them money, and be a powerful recruitment tool.

Cigna Corporation, an insurance company in Philadelphia, reports that it saves $240,000 a year in reduced health insurance premiums for its employees by promoting breastfeeding among its employees—plus another $60,000 in reduced absenteeism costs. That's because breastfed babies generally suffer fewer illnesses and require less medical care. Breastfed babies require 62 percent fewer prescription medicines than other infants. And healthy babies mean that parents can show up at work, rather than stay home and take care of a sick child.

Cigna initiated a program that provides lactation rooms, with pumps, sinks, and refrigerators, as well as the right to take a break and use those rooms. Not surprisingly, women at Cigna are far more likely to succeed at breastfeeding than working moms at less supportive companies. More than 70 percent of the moms enrolled in the program were still nursing when their babies were six months old, compared to only

20 percent of all working moms. At a year, 36 percent of Cigna moms in the program were breastfeeding, compared to the national average of only 10 percent of all working moms.

The size of the savings at a company like Cigna can sway almost any thoughtful employer to provide you with breaks during the day for expressing milk, if nothing else.

Breastfeeding advocates point out that granting breaks to nursing moms should be standard at all American companies, especially since most allow employees to take breaks to smoke cigarettes! That is, in fact, an argument a few moms have used to their advantage. "When my boss resisted, I just pointed out to him that I would probably spend about the same amount of time expressing milk as the smokers at the company spent outside killing themselves. He didn't give me any trouble after that," says Clare, who works at a firm in the Midwest.

Yet it is pathetic that American women have to use smokers' breaks as a justification for being allowed to take time to express milk for their babies. At least that is the consensus of a growing number of advocates, who are trying to bring American business into the new millennium on breastfeeding and work.

Trying to Improve the Situation

In fact, lots more needs to be done to help American mothers juggle breastfeeding and their jobs. Even with the endorsement of breastfeeding by doctors and the lip service paid to the need for babies to stay connected to their mothers during the first year, most American employers still do very little to help moms continue nursing after their return to work, even though their needs are very modest. "Women who wish to continue breastfeeding after returning to work have relatively few needs: availability of dependable, efficient breast pumps; a clean, convenient, safe, and private location to express milk at the worksite; the opportunity to pump frequently enough to maintain their milk supply; and an adequate place to store their milk," says Carolyn Maloney, U.S. congresswoman from New York, who has proposed amendments to the Pregnancy Discrimination Act that would offer just such support to women.

Many advocates believe such a law is way overdue, given the hostile way that some working women have been treated. Some have been harassed or even fired for trying to express milk during work hours, even when they did it during a bone fide lunch break or another legal break time. Several high-profile cases have even made it to U.S. district courts over the last decade, but there has been no conclusive ruling to protect all women's rights. That's why Carolyn Maloney has proposed the amendment to the Pregnancy Discrimination Act, and other lawmakers have proposed or even passed laws to protect nursing mothers at the state level.

Such laws are on the books in other industrialized countries, along with those generous maternity leaves and family allowances that help working parents raise healthy, happy children. "It's so disgraceful that mothers in this country still lack even basic support for continuing to breastfeed when they get back to work. In fact, some meet with open hostility, and so far, the courts don't always support their cause," says Elizabeth Baldwin, a Florida attorney who handles such issues for La Leche League. "Other countries fully support working mothers, requiring employers to give women the time and space to express milk. It's shameful that we are so far behind."

A FEW GOOD COMPANIES
FOR NURSING MOTHERS

A few companies now have special rooms and equipment for women who want to keep nursing when they get back to work. Nine were recently honored by the National Healthy Mothers, Healthy Babies Coalition: Aetna, Hartford, Connecticut; Cigna Corporation, Philadelphia; Eastman Kodak, Rochester, New York; Johns Hopkins University, Baltimore; Kaiser Permanente, Hawaii; Lincoln Financial Group, Philadelphia; Los Angeles Department of Power and Water; Patagonia, Ventura, California; and PricewaterhouseCoopers in New York City.

LA LECHE LEAGUE

Help!

So you thought breastfeeding would be the most natural thing in the world—and now you find out it's more confusing than rocket science. (If only you knew rocket science.)

Your baby won't latch on to the nipple. Or your nipples are so sore that you don't want your baby to latch on. Your milk supply is too little. Your milk supply is too much.

What to do?

Don't despair. Visit the La Leche League's Web site (www.lalecheleague.org) to find a chapter near you, or just to browse for tips. This group, dedicated to the promotion and support of breastfeeding, has been around for decades. It was founded at a time when breastfeeding had fallen out of favor has remained a vital source of support for breastfeeding moms around the world. (The name La Leche League is derived from the French word for milk, *lait*.)

If you want a lactation consultant to work with you, the local chapter can probably recommend one. Local hospitals, midwives or your local health department can also help you find one. If you go that route, make sure that she has been certified by the International Board of Lactation Consultant Examiners.

STATES THAT SMILE ON BREASTFEEDING MOMS

As more and more women try to continue nursing when they return to work, some employers have resisted, and breastfeeding has become a legal issue. A few women have even been reprimanded or threatened with loss of their jobs for taking a break to express milk. That's why a growing number of state legislatures have taken steps to support and protect working mothers who continue to breastfeed. Here are the most helpful, as of 2001:

California: Legislators passed a resolution in 1998 encouraging employers to support and encourage breastfeeding by providing a place where employees can express milk, store it, or even bring their babies to nurse them, on breaks.

Florida: Back in 1994, state legislators passed one of the most sweeping laws to support breastfeeding moms. The state has committed itself to developing written policies for the workplace that address such issues as flexibility in schedules to accommodate nursing moms, creation of breaks for pumping and expressing, and providing private places for employees to express milk, which include a sink and a place to store breast milk safely.

Georgia: The state senate passed a bill that encourages employers to establish programs and policies that support breastfeeding moms.

Hawaii: The state house of representatives is considering a bill that would require the state Civil Rights Commission to publish data about examples of discrimination related to breastfeeding or expressing milk in the workplace.

Illinois: A Nursing Mothers in the Workplace Act was introduced which would require that companies provide reasonable, unpaid break time and a space to women who need to express milk.

Maryland: Legislators proposed in recent years that employers who create a supportive environment for nursing moms be allowed to declare themselves "family-friendly" in promotional brochures.

Minnesota: Employers must provide reasonable, unpaid break time each day to women who want to express milk—as long as such breaks do not disrupt the firm's operations.

New Mexico: Legislators are considering the New Mothers Breastfeeding Promotion and Protection Act, which bans employers from discriminating against nursing moms. Employers who support breastfeeding moms could collect tax credits for such things as supplying pumps or lactation consultants or creating a permanent lactation room.

Texas: Like Maryland, state legislators here passed a bill that gives employers who encourage breastfeeding the right to use a special designation, in this case, "mother-friendly," in promotional materials aimed at recruiting new workers or boosting the company image. The bill also set up worksite breastfeeding support policies for all state employees.

Chapter 5

Home with Your New Baby

When spring came, Mary came out of her house across the street, and we talked in person for the first time in months. We'd had five or six major nor'easters blow through, snow on the ground since December, and she had two kids under the age of two. The baby had had colic for weeks and weeks. She'd called me several times, desperate for ideas to soothe him, and I'd given her every single tip I'd ever heard. The only thing that worked was the hair dryer, turning on the hair dryer next to him while he was in his infant seat. Then Thomas would be quiet for fifteen minutes at a time. For Mary, a blessed fifteen minutes.

This beautiful spring day, Mary bounded out the door, carrying now-smiling and beatific baby Tommy, and negotiating with two-year-old Michael and her black Labrador retriever, still a puppy, who was leaping all over them.

Yes, a seventy-pound puppy and two kids under the age of two.

This is the insanity we visit on ourselves, by choice. Once you get the kids, the dogs often follow, along with the new house, and a million other changes. Station wagons, mini-vans, playsets in the backyard.

But no one really expects to spend months indoors with a baby who is spasmodically crying. Mary was exuberant to be outside at last, giddy and radiant with sun on her face.

"Lucky to be alive, right?" I joked with her.

"I'm so happy to be alive today," she said.

"No, that's not what I meant," I replied, and paused for a minute. "I mean, the kids. *They* are lucky to be alive, right? You guys made it through the winter."

She laughed so hard she nearly wet her pants. "You're right about that," she said. Coming from a large Catholic family who loves babies, Mary would never make such a confession lightly. But being a shut-in with her infant son for the winter had taken its toll. There'd been days she'd wanted to chuck it all, she said. Go away for a week. A month.

Or more!

She laughed again, out loud, a little hysterical at her own admission.

"Yep," she said. "You are definitely right. *They* are lucky to be alive."

Mary's early days with her son were quite different from my own maternity leaves. I had both my kids in the summer, when even the worst days had the redemption of long hours of sunlight and gentle balmy evenings. And neither of my children had colic. Like many newborns, Rachel was fussy in the evenings, for about three weeks, off and on. But unlike so many colicky babies, she could be soothed. She didn't cry as long as she was perched on my shoulder, and I kept moving. So every night for those three weeks, I took Rachel for what I came to call "shoulder rides."

No one can accurately predict just how your first mater-nity leave will go. Or your second. No two leaves are alike, even for the same woman. That's because no two babies are the same, nor is your family, the circumstances of your job—heck, you may not even have the same job—or your finances. Your marriage, your friends, your neighbors, your support network, and your feelings about juggling work and motherhood also change from year to year, even month to month. And all these things color your adjustment—especially the first time out.

Your first leave can be delicious. "I loved my first maternity leave," says Jess, "and I was very surprised at how much I loved it. I found the first few months with a new baby to be a very special, magical time. With my first child, I was amazed at how much I loved this little bundle." She liked it so much, in fact, that she did it three more times! Now the mother of four, she swears that maternity leave simply "put everything in perspective."

That may happen to you. But I suggest that you prepare for a winter like Mary's, just in case you have to endure one. Most of us find the first leave the most trying. "I always tell new moms to be prepared for a very rough start," says another woman, who's also a lawyer. "It's hard to imagine what it's like to go without a good night's sleep for weeks on end. In retrospect, I'd say they were wonderful weeks. But at the time, I remember I was also tired, bored, and cranky, with fairly low self-esteem. I remember a few nights when I woke with the baby, nursed her, and then just cried from exhaustion."

It helps to get some idea of what you're in for, adjusting your expectations and adopting strategies that make life easier. That way, you can gloat if things go as well as they did for Jess during her first maternity leave. But if you're not that lucky, you'll ensure that both you and your baby do come out alive, ready for the next twenty-one years!

Your Confidence Will Plummet

The first thing to expect after giving birth is that you will be rendered temporarily stupid. As far as I can tell, no one escapes this unsettled state of mind. I call it new-mommy-itis, a state of mind that makes you not just insecure but helplessly and hopelessly insecure.

This comes as a sharp contrast to your experience on the job, when you confidently paddled through the days, knowing just what to expect and what to do. Now you are utterly unable to trust your own judgment and ready to accept just about anyone else's. You actively seek counsel from total strangers, people whom you might have dismissed as clueless just last month—the columnists in magazines, guests on television talk shows, parenting "experts" at remote Internet sites, that neighbor you've hardly spoken to before, friends who have always turned to *you* for help. Even your husband's cousin, whom you found insufferable because of her opinions on politics, art, movies and women's place in the world. Now you are *happy* when she calls, because she had a baby last year and knows everything, *everything* about breastfeeding.

Well, just relax and accept this temporary lapse in confidence. It will pass. In a few months, in fact, you'll be the expert on your baby, bossing everyone around as if *they* are the ignoramuses. You'll have definite opinions on whether to use cloth or disposable diapers, whether parents should offer a pacifier or encourage thumb-sucking, whether to pick up the baby every time he whimpers or let him cry it out.

But for now, just realize that in the first few weeks, it's absolutely natural to feel inept, to second-guess yourself and wonder whether you are doing the right thing. These feelings are a barometer of both the deep love you feel for your baby and the deep change in your life. Suddenly, everyone's calling you Mom and expecting you to know what's best for this tiny and precious being. Even when she's screaming and everything you've tried, including the hair dryer, has failed.

"Becoming a new parent is a giant step, a huge transition, and many women are overwhelmed at times by the power of the emotions that come with this change," says Ellen Galinsky, president of the Families and Work Institute and author of the *Six Stages of Parenting.* "Suddenly, they feel both very insecure and very possessive of their new babies. They want to do the right thing, but they aren't always sure what that right thing is. It can feel very confusing, especially when the baby is crying and you can't calm her down. Or when you're trying to nurse and she won't take the breast. It's not surprising that new mothers report many mood swings in those early days, from euphoria to upset, even in the space of a few hours."

Also, you haven't slept. And if you are truly inexperienced in the baby-care department, then you do truly need help. From anyone able to teach you. "When my sister and I first brought Justin home, we both realized we didn't know how to change this little guy's diaper right," Wendy says. "He'd been on an intensive-care unit, so we didn't even do changes in the hospital. My sister and I had him on the floor at home, and we were trying to figure out what to do when the twelve-year-old neighbor boy came over to visit with us. Jeremiah had taken a 'parenting class' in his school. He showed us how to put Justin's diaper on! Three cheers for those classes!"

You can sign up for classes yourself at the local church, hospital, YWCA, or community center; join a new mother's circle; hire a baby nurse; or just find a friend to walk you through Baby Basics. How to change diapers. How to burp the baby. How to get that nightgown on and off. But for most of us, the mechanics of parenthood are the least of it. It's the flood of feelings, from sheer delight when you hold those little fingers and toes to sheer helplessness and fear the first time she spikes a fever.

What my friends and I have discovered is that what helps the most is to accept the intensity of it all, try to maintain a sense of humor, get some sleep, and just believe that those bad first days will pass. They will. And that you'll learn as you go. We all do.

"My first leave was fairly traumatic for the first few months because, well, let's face it, I didn't know what in God's name I was doing," says Sarah. "I cried and cried the whole way home from the hospital and continued for a few days. Then the baby had colic for three months straight. I was nothing short of a basket case until he calmed down, and then I did, too. With my second child, I just didn't get that rattled. I'd seen diaper rash, been through colic, fevers, teething, the whole thing. I enjoyed it the second time around so much more. I felt like I knew what I was doing. Or at least that most of the things I'd worried about the first time didn't matter that much."

Another friend echoes her sentiments. "Oh, I was so nervous with my first that I hardly got out of the house. We spent most of my maternity leave inside. With my second, I had a great time. I learned to load him up and take him with me everywhere. I knew he was going to be fine. I felt very liberated just by knowing what to expect. I wish someone had told me to calm down the first time around."

Lower Your Expectations

It also helps to have realistic expectations of your maternity leave. That is, expect to do nothing except care for the baby.

Everyone will tell you this, and hopefully you will listen. I did not, of course. As I revealed a few pages back, on my first maternity leave I decided to make curtains for my the baby's room. And a quilt. These were really dumb projects for maternity leave, but such optimism as to how much we can accomplish is typical among the friends I've checked with. For many of us, the nesting instinct takes over in late pregnancy, and with gusto. Perfectly rational women I know suddenly launch ambitious, undoable home decoration projects, intending to complete them "while the baby sleeps." They are still in that state of mind we all have on the job: enjoying the unfettered belief that we can actually make a plan and carry it out.

Then you discover how ridiculous it is to try to get anything done. Nearly every time I got out the sewing machine and the fabric, Rachel woke up. So I decided I would just leave the sewing machine out, with plans to complete those curtains in short spurts. Given that I had only a few seams and hems to sew, this did not seem very ambitious to my pre-mother self. Or even to my very greenhorn-mother self. But even one seam proved overwhelming. No matter when I sat down I was tired and my eyes were bleary and then Rae would start to cry, and I'd make a mistake that I'd have to rip out. I did finish them, out of some stubborn, dogged determination. But the fabric for the quilt went into a box and didn't come out again until she reached grade school. We used swatches of it for art projects.

So I hope you'll pay attention to what I'm saying here. It's one piece of advice that is really, truly useful. Lower your expectations. Expect to get nothing, absolutely nothing, done on maternity leave, except taking care of your baby. Don't even aspire to do the small stuff if you can get someone else to. Don't wash the dishes the first week. In fact, don't use dishes, if you can avoid it. Use paper plates and cups. Have your husband, friend, mother, mother-in-law, sister, neighbor, or Significant Other bring in takeout. And then take out what's left of the take-out to the garbage.

I'm not kidding about this. In those first weeks, you'll be surprised at how much time it takes to care for a newborn. "The element that was most stunning to me about having a new baby was how much time it consumed," said Susie. "I remember feeling dumbfounded at the end of a day when I sat there knowing that I had been incredibly busy, but really couldn't name anything substantial that I had accomplished. No meals cooked, really, no shower, no housework, no reading. I think the time breastfeeding consumes is something you don't expect until you experience it. It just seems constant in the beginning."

Similarly, another friend confesses that she'd had an "extraordinarily unrealistic view of what maternity leave would be. I thought I'd be sipping coffee and sitting on the front stoop, taking long walks, giggles, long naps, and get this one: piano lessons—at least once a week. So it was a huge reality check when I would find myself still in my pajamas at six p.m., usually without a shirt because I'd get so sick of yanking it up and down all day to nurse and pump. No shower, no washed dishes, stacks of magazines I didn't get close to reading," she says.

Part of the reason babies take so much time is that most of them don't believe in long naps. They do sleep, just as the books tell you, for upwards of ten, twelve, fourteen, even sixteen hours a day. Just not all at once. A few minutes of shut-eye is plenty for most of them, and then they need you again. And you never know when it's going to happen. "I had figured the baby would sleep a lot so I signed up for two summer classes at school. I also brought some work home from the plant that I was planning to complete. I realized pretty quickly that, yes, babies do sleep a lot, but they do it in ten-minute chunks. School was a struggle, and I never got around to the work I brought home from my job," says Tanya, who works for a big chemical company.

So accept the early chaos—and take some solace in knowing that it will end. Your baby will settle, probably after the first three or four weeks, and the demands will slow. She'll figure out the difference between night and day. Naps, feedings, and even the fussy times will start to happen at more regular intervals during the day. But in the beginning, you'll do yourself a favor if you consider it a victory to get dressed, brush your hair, and shower. If you accept this standard, you'll feel like a genius if you do one more thing. Like wash the dishes or go for a walk.

And bear in mind that there are rewards on the other side of the early chaos. Everyone will tell you that life changes when your baby smiles at you (which may happen as soon as at three weeks), and it's true. Suddenly, you let go of much of the exhaustion and hard work you did to get to this point. You'll settle yourself into your new role as mother. "I found early motherhood to be brutal. In fact, I thought I'd go insane," says Martha. "So I was also surprised at how much I've come to love being a mother. I don't want to sound like a sappy Hallmark card, but I am moved to tears by the little things he does. I am mesmerized by his appearance, his gestures, his abilities, and his emerging personality. I have never been so delighted to put something to bed, and then I can't wait to get him up and do it all over again."

Getting Help

Given the constant demands of a baby, nearly everyone will tell you to get some help—from a friend, a sister, a mother-in-law, a baby nurse, anyone who can lend a hand in the first week or two. And that is a very good idea.

My own mother came across the continent for the first few weeks after Rachel was born, and her help and support were invaluable. She was no spring chicken herself, but she stayed a week and did a lot of little things, like the baby's wash, making dinner, and buying groceries. Just having another adult in the house so I could really nap without worrying about Rachel meant a lot.

If you don't have family nearby, you might consider hiring some help, if it won't break the bank. After Dan was born, I hired a high school girl to come in for a few hours a day, a few days a week for a couple of weeks, just to play with Rachel while I nursed Dan. Sometimes she even ran a few errands for me.

I know other friends who've even used "doulas," women who are trained to help you with childbirth, breastfeeding, and the adjustment at home. The term "doula" comes from the Greek word for female slave—the doula was, in fact, the most important female serving woman in a household.

The modern-day doula plays an important, supportive role for new mothers. She will see you through childbirth, offering massages and emotional support, and even bringing you chunks of ice or lemonade or whatever you want to get through labor. After you give birth, she will come to your house for a couple hours a day, for a few days a week, for as long as you need her. She's trained to teach you about baby care, help you get comfortable as you recover, fill you in on what to expect during recovery, teach you about how to care for a newborn, and do most anything else you need, even run errands or put in a load of wash. Doulas are among the few beings on earth who pay more than lip service to motherhood, giving you both the practical and emotional support you need as you ease into your new role. To find a doula, visit the Doulas of North America's homepage at www.dona.org, or ask your pediatrician or hospital for referrals.

My own mom hired "baby nurses" through agencies that specialize in finding domestic help for families. These women often show up in white uniforms, with white shoes, like home health-care workers. Many see their job as caring primarily for the baby, which is not surprising, given the name of their profession. Yet, from what I hear from friends, that is the aspect of their help that can be supremely annoying, especially if you are nursing the baby yourself. The baby nurse can end up taking over the baby instead of staying supportively in the background while you gain confidence.

What most of us want in the beginning is someone to support us, help around the house, and take on the baby in a pinch. That's why doulas sound so much more appealing to me; the goal of their profession is mother support, not baby care.

But a few of my friends swear by the baby nurses they hired. The trick, they insist, is to interview the person and lay out upfront what you want. You can find the agencies who provide baby nurses under "child care" in the Yellow Pages.

When Visitors Arrive

Just as you are dialing for help, however, you may be interrupted by all those other people who are dialing to congratulate you. The neighbors. Your aunts. Your cousins. Your husband's aunts. Your husband's cousins. Your coworkers. Your husband's coworkers. Your friends from out of town. Your friends in town.

And they are showing up. Right at the front door. Without calling first.

That's right. Babies are a magnet for everybody. And no wonder. Who else has those little toes and fingers? That soft skin? Childbirth is an event everyone can celebrate, newborns are people everyone wants to cuddle, and so they will. They want to congratulate you, and they want to see the baby.

And hold the baby. And play with the baby. And talk about the baby.

And then talk to you about *their* baby. Even if their baby is now forty or fifty years old. Seeing a newborn just brings it all back. And they're ready to share it with you in detail.

And all of this is happening just when the baby, your baby, that is, has finally fallen asleep—and you're ready to take a nap. You realize this just as they really get into their stories.

Still, you don't see this coming. You're so excited yourself at first, that you just go to the door. You're excited to see how excited they are. And they've brought you a gift!

If you're as silly as I was, and so many other first-time mothers I know, you'll put on a pot of coffee, scrounge around for some cookies to put on a plate. Then you'll sit down, rip open the gift, and start to gab.

Only to find, about three minutes into the visit, that this was a big mistake. All you want to do is lie down and go to sleep. You can't hear a word they are saying. You can't wait for them to leave. You have never been this tired. Bone-deep tired.

And now the baby is crying.

So what to do?

Get through this visit as best you can, and then never do it again.

Okay, if you're like me, you may have to endure two or three of these visits to learn the lesson. Or you could just heed this advice now.

Whenever you come to your senses, do adopt these policies: Do not answer the door, do not answer the phone, do not let anyone into your house during the first week at home after the birth, and maybe even the second and third, except at the hours and under the circumstances that work for you. You might, for example, only see friends and even relatives on the weekends, when your husband is home to help. When he's home, you can politely excuse yourself if you need to, and go take a nap. Your spouse and the visitors can happily entertain and soothe the baby.

You can relay the important facts about your baby to well-wishers via your phone answering machine. Leave a message with all the vital statistics—the baby's sex, name, birth weight, and anything else you want the world to know. Make it silly and fun, so people don't feel annoyed that you aren't answering the phone. And let everyone know that you can't wait to talk to them—just not right at this moment. Then unplug the phone, let the machine take the messages, and call back when you're ready.

Accept the Initial Loss of Control

Taking control of these small things can help because in general, you'll find that you don't have control over much in the first month or so at home. The days are simply unpredictable at first, and it will boost your mental health if you can embrace this fact, rather than fight it.

But for many working women, this is the hardest reality of all. We're used to days that have some definition and structure, adult conversation, concrete accomplishments, and some feedback on how we're doing. Time to go to the bathroom, for God's sake.

Life with a new baby offers none of that. Some days, the only feedback we get is from a tiny person wailing at us, telling us for the third time today that we really don't know what we are doing. (That's the part we're still trying to figure out. Teething? Hungry? Tired? Cold coming on?)

And maternity leave is also different because it's just not like any other period in your life. Not only are you not in control of this little baby, but you aren't really in control of much of anything for the moment. You're suspended from your normal life and normal routines. You're not a stay-at-home mom, ready to turn the rhythm and content of these days at home into the rest of your life. You're in transition. You are only home temporarily, trying to recover and get this baby off to a good start. Everything is new, and everything is unpredictable. Basically, your baby is in the driver's seat and you are holding on for dear life, hoping someone gets some driving lessons soon!

You may not even know how you're going to get from morning to night most days. Not that you don't make plans. As a working woman, you're used to having a plan for every day, so that's how you start out. You plan to get to the grocery store, for example. Filling the fridge might give you a real sense of accomplishment. But you abandon that plan because your baby is fussy. Or because she fell asleep unexpectedly and you're deeply grateful to have a little time to yourself.

Then there are the larger issues that are just now coming onto your radar screen. Having this baby really is going to change everything. People told you this, and now you're starting to get it. Your husband went back to work, probably, and parachuted back into his pre-dad life. But not you. You see that for you, this baby is going to affect everything, from the small stuff, like getting out of the house, to the big stuff, like buying a house in a district with good schools. Whether you can successfully balance the needs of this baby with the demands of your job. It's beginning to dawn on you, all of this. You feel the big change in your bones.

"The biggest surprise of all was the loss of control," says Kathy, who works in advertising and had been accustomed to controlling just about everything in her life. "No longer are you the queen of your schedule or your bank account. Once the supreme ruler of time and money, suddenly you have no control over any of it." Suddenly, she even lost control over the time when she could take a shower. Like many of us, she learned to think of it all as a trade-off. "When you look at the baby, you're willing to give up that queen status. Most of the time, you just accept that your needs are going to take second place to this new little person that you love dearly. It's just that before she arrives, you didn't realize it would mean that you wouldn't get to sip coffee and read the paper on Sunday morning."

Your sense of dwindling control will be even more acute if you are strapped for cash, the baby was not planned, or you must live with some other circumstance not of your choosing. "I turned twenty-four a few days after my son was born and I was a basket case during most of my leave. I had no money to do anything or go anywhere and no other stay-at-home moms to spend time with. It was a very long six months. My husband would come home from work and I'd pass the baby off to him and walk out of the house," says my friend Terri. "I never had any babysitting experience and now I was a mother! Compared to working a regular full-time job, motherhood was really hard for me. I missed the adult interaction and mental stimulation on the job."

Michelle was actually pleased to get calls from her boss during maternity leave, commenting, "I think because I had worked for so many years before I had my baby, I found it very difficult to stay home every day, without any real structure. At work, you can see a project through and can measure your accomplishments readily. In the house, I was getting depressed and obsessed with trying to keep the house neat and orderly. So I liked getting the calls from work, because my boss's questions were so straightforward, I could answer them and it made me feel competent again, as if I had some control over things."

For most of us, a call from the boss would not add to the sense of control (just the opposite, I suspect!). But Michelle's reaction illustrates the contrast so many of us feel between our working lives and caring for a baby. Maternity leave is just the beginning of the new balancing act, of learning how to adapt to the very different demands of being a parent and those of being a worker. Being a mom means diving into life as a process, without having any clear goals. Being a worker means setting goals all the time, and achieving them.

Over time, you'll find your own balance and regain a sense of control. You'll have your routines at home and your accomplishments at work, and you'll learn to gerrymander between them, stretching the boundaries when you have to, to make it all work. Each of my friends has learned to make it work in different ways.

Michelle ended up going back to work sooner than she'd planned, just to get out of the house. "My husband suggested it. He could just see how frazzled and depressed I was getting at home. So I called my boss and we worked out a part-time arrangement, which is just perfect. I needed to be somewhere with structure, at least part of the day."

For other moms, relinquishing control, accepting the lack of structure, at least for maternity leave, is what works best. "Okay, I admit it. I just gave up," says Margaret. "I just said to myself, dirty dishes don't matter, dirty clothes don't matter. All that matters is taking care of the baby, and that's all I'm going to do. I was much happier then."

Get on Schedule

That's not to say that you could or should spend your entire maternity leave with the white flag run up the flagpole. Instead, you learn that much of parenting is all in the timing. The first few weeks require that you relinquish control, much as they advise in all twelve-step programs. I've always thought they should have one of those programs for new parents, to teach us to accept the things we can't control, and change the ones we can.

But after those initial terrorizing days of being on call 24/7, life does change. Your child begins to have some focus and control over her own body, needs, and wants. As she matures, she'll emerge from the chaos, and so will you. She'll go longer between feedings, won't fuss as much, and will allow you to calm her.

And then, as with breastfeeding, you'll start to create a dance for your days, a two-step that you master together, based on your baby's needs and yours, colored by both of your personalities. By about six weeks, you'll even begin to see who your child is. You'll discover if you have a sleeper or an insomniac. (I had one of each.) Or if you have a big eater, a snacker, or someone in between. An outgoing or a shy guy.

And then you'll begin to know what to do. How often to feed, when to play, how to play, when to nap. In fact, that veil of stupidity lifts and you'll find yourself more confident, telling other people just how to handle your baby, how to talk to him, how to soothe his jangled nerves. And you'll have more fun. "I remember when Jeremy started laughing at the mobile over his crib. I'd spin it and he'd laugh. It was as if, after all those fussy nights, we'd started to talk—even though he never said a word. Everything got easier after that," says Stephanie.

At this point you can finally assert some control, establishing some routines and guiding your baby into behavior that works not only for her but for the whole household. It's your first foray into the skills that will help you as a working mom, because as life goes on, you'll live and die by routines and schedules. They just make life easier and healthier, for both you and your baby. At first, you'll start to set patterns for sleeping and eating. Later on, it's lining up the lunch boxes, signing the school notices, and having the gloves and hats in a basket by the door.

Sometimes you recognize the need for this on your own. And sometimes, someone gives you a nudge. Whatever the case, pay attention. "When my son was about three months old, a more experienced mother I hardly knew just took one look at me and said, 'You look terrible! Are you okay?'" recalls my friend Chris. "I told her I hadn't slept more than three hours at a stretch for three months—and she told me it was time to get my baby on a schedule.

"Once she said it, I thought, yes! Yes, that's exactly what I need to do. So I started to let my son cry it out a little at night, instead of getting up at every whimper. And sure enough, within a month we were on a schedule." In some ways, she's astonished that it didn't occur to her sooner, but she adds, "I think the general anxiety of being a new mother and not getting enough sleep really took its toll. I was a walking zombie. I couldn't think things through, and I don't think he was ready yet. But once he got on a schedule and I got some sleep, I began to feel human again."

Don't Go Through It Alone

As you feel human, you may also feel the need for a new social life, if you haven't already. In fact, as the weeks pass on maternity leave, you're going to want friends more than ever. Especially other new moms who can empathize with what you're going through. People who will be happy to talk about diapers, burping, strollers, high chairs, and all the rest with abandon. People who know this stuff is not boring, but the very essence of life for the moment. People you can giggle with, blow off steam with, admit that your baby drives you crazy even though you love him.

This isn't just fun, it's essential to your mental health. Nancy Marshall, a psychologist and researcher at Wellesley College, has found that having a network of friends is a key predictor of a working mom's adjustment. "Women who had someone to talk to, to share their worries and concerns with, were much less likely to get depressed or feel overwhelmed," she says.

No surprise there for most of us, when we stop to think about it. Life on maternity leave is almost a recipe for depression. Psychologists have long identified such factors as a loss of control, isolation, lack of concrete accomplishments, and ignoring personal needs as contributors to poor mental health. And studies do show that more than half of all new moms suffer some form of passing depression and anxiety in the first few weeks at home. It makes sense, given the magnitude of the change in your life and the new demands on your time and emotions.

But in the company of friends, most of us do fine. Just knowing that everyone feels the same way helps. My friends who didn't find a circle of new moms tell me they wish they had. "My husband traveled a lot for his job, which made my isolation even worse than it is for most moms on maternity leave," says Ruth. "I wished I'd joined a group for new mothers in the time I was home. I often offer that advice to first-time moms in similar circumstances."

Ditto, says Bonnie. "I basically just sat around the house all day and grew lonelier and more isolated. Although my family came by frequently to visit, I didn't have the companionship of many friends. I was the first to have children in my circle and so no one was interested in mine," she says. "Needless to say, I was very happy to get back to work and be surrounded again with other adults."

You can join a group for new mothers at a church, the local Y, or through your pediatrician, your hospital, or a local community center. The great thing about these groups is that you'll be in the company of women who are struggling with and genuinely interested in the same things you are: How *do* you get the baby to burp? What brand of diapers don't ever leak?

It's even better if you can find a group of women on maternity leave who share the added concern about how in the world they are going to get back to work. Together, you can talk about child care, husbands, and bosses and figure out how to weather what comes next. What you're going to want more than anything is support and help as you fashion your new family and get back to work.

SCHWA, N M

40348

Saturday, October 28, 2017

BABY BLUES

In a way, it's amazing that every mom doesn't suffer from postpartum depression. After all, we have to cope with all the factors that are associated with poor mental health: loss of control, lack of sleep, unending demands, erratic behavior, no time for ourselves.

Some studies show that as many as 50 to 75 percent of all new moms do experience at least a passing form of depression in the first few weeks at home. You may cry for no reason you can name, or be restless, impatient, irritable, or unreasonably anxious. Doctors call this the "baby blues," and it passes.

But for some women, the feelings persist and become overwhelming. Many women report that the depression just creeps up on them, in the midst of all the other changes in their lives. "I suffered from the baby blues and had no idea what that was," says Barbara, a hairdresser. "I was crying as much as the baby was! I felt out of control, lost, and frustrated."

Like many new moms, she'd read every magazine and baby book she could lay her hands on, only to feel that she wasn't measuring up when things didn't go well at home. "At least at work, I knew how to be successful. The mom thing wasn't so easy. I felt like a failure because all the magazines talk about bonding with the baby and how great it is."

"Well, for me, it was not great at first and nobody had given me any straight talk about how hard it would be some days," she says. Like so many mothers, she's always reluctant to concede that she had such hard days, for fear people will think she doesn't love her baby.

"Don't get me wrong," she adds quickly. "It is a beautiful experience, and very rewarding. In the long run." Then she pauses and ads, "But some days it sucks!"

With money worries, and a husband who wasn't helping much, her days got worse before they got better, until she talked over her moods with her doctor. She did have a classic case of postpartum depression, one that passed when the maternity leave was over. But getting on medication and some counseling helped see her through the dark days.

Postpartum depression is characterized by sadness, a feeling of hopelessness, poor appetite, uncontrolled crying, or irritability that persists for a few weeks or more without relief. Sometimes the depression expresses itself more as anxiety, with moments of panic, shakiness, dizziness, or a rapidly beating heart. If you suspect you are suffering from postpartum depression, don't wait—consult your doctor.

Chapter 6

Now You're Both Parents—
Or Are You?

W hen Lucy, a professor, had her first child, her husband had a classic male reaction.

He ran for the hills.

Well, more accurately, he ran for his workshop, where he repairs pianos for a living. There, he began to put in twelve-to fourteen-hour days for the first few weeks after the baby was born. When he was home, which seemed like never to Lucy, he was irritable and tense. "Harsh," Lucy says. "I would use the word 'harsh,' which was just not like him. He's usually a pretty easy-going guy."

He was also suddenly and intensely preoccupied with money. "All he could think of was whether we'd be able to pay for college tuition—and Rory was exactly one week old. One week old!" says Lucy. "And he was worried about paying for college!"

Unlike many of us, Lucy was empathetic and gentle about her husband's withdrawal. And highly perceptive. "It was pretty clear to me what was going on," she says. "He was acting this way because he was so nervous. It was *his* form of postpartum depression, his reaction to having a new baby and all that responsibility."

Not that she didn't have her own feelings about the way her mate was acting. "I felt deserted. I was upset and angry," she concedes. But they had a marriage where they could talk things through. "I reminded him that he'd just had an incredible year financially, and asked him why he was so freaked about money," she said. "I knew we were going to do fine."

And she told him in no uncertain terms that she needed him. "I just told him he was going to have to calm down and stop acting with such hysteria," she says. "I needed him here. Rory needed him here."

That straightforward approach worked. It could be that all he needed was some reassurance. Many men feel left out after the baby arrives, especially if you are nursing. And most of us need to be reassured about money, once that tiny, new dependent being arrives in our lives. Whatever the reason, within a few days of their conversation, Lucy's husband changed his workaholic ways and began to spend more time at home. Which turned out to be mostly wonderful. They even made it out to a duck pond for a picnic on a warm autumn day.

"Before Rory was born, we had talked about the idea of new adventures, that this baby was going to bring new excitement to our lives," Lucy recalls. "It's true that she has done that. She's enriched our lives in many ways, just making us slow down and pay attention to what's all around us."

Anxiety on the Loose

As Lucy found out, babies do bring adventure to marriage, although not always the kind of adventure you imagined at that riveting moment you discovered you were pregnant. At that moment, you pictured the new family, the perfect family, the family who grew close and loving together. Sunning yourselves on the beach on Cape Cod, tasting the salt, feeling the gritty sand on your feet, admiring your child's tanned skin and smiling face. Laughing at the chocolate pudding all over your toddler's face and hands.

Your husband teaching your daughter how to fish. You teaching your son how to cook. (Okay, I'm a child of the sixties, and a feminist. That was my fantasy.)

Fabulous picnics at the zoo, restful drives in the country. Together, teaching your child how to ride a bike.

All in good time. These things are all possible in good time. But as maternity leave begins, your adventures may be more like Lucy's, both more vexing and bracing than you expected, challenging your marriage to change and adapt to the new circumstances that "baby makes three." And you have to ride through the changes even though you and your husband may be acting out weird anxieties that you've never even seen before. Like Lucy's husband suddenly camping out at his workshop. I panicked when my husband left the hospital after Rachel was delivered, certain that he'd died in a car accident or been mugged. I insisted the nurses get me to a phone, even though I was still on the labor and delivery ward, so I could call him. He was in the shower, and had to get out to answer the phone.

The first few days at home, I wept for no known reason, even though I felt happier than I'd ever been in my life. A week later, I left the car keys in the freezer, creating a mini-crisis when I needed to get to the pediatrician. This sort of behavior does not make marriage an easy contract. And I've learned, from friends and the experts, that I was hardly alone in my zaniness.

Newborns make many people nervous, especially those who've had very little experience holding, soothing, or diapering one. Which covers most men. Even those of us who grew up caring for younger siblings can testify to the terror of holding a tiny screaming baby in your arms who simply refuses to be comforted. Especially when you are trying to come to terms with the fact that this relationship will last for the rest of your life. "I know it sounds silly," says Marcy. "But there were moments where I really didn't believe that he'd stop crying. Or walk. Or get toilet trained. The first time around, you just lose all perspective. And you get crazy. Sometimes, I'd just hand Tom the baby when he walked in the door from work, and walk right out the door."

Many men act as Lucy's husband did, though perhaps not so extreme. They find solace in work. The environment is familiar, predictable, and the adults there really do seem to be in charge. (Even when they really aren't, many pretend to be.) There's no squalor, no dirty diapers, no dirty dishes, no one trying out their brand-new lungs. In fact, one of my psychologist friends tells me it's absolutely normal for many men to flee to work in the early days after the baby is born. "It's not just an escape, it's also fulfilling the traditional role," he says. "Men still get lots of points for being the Family Provider, just as women score lots of points for staying home with the baby and being the Good Mother. Going to work is what men are still supposed to do in our culture; it's what's expected. And doing what's expected can be very reassuring when you're living through a big change, like becoming a new parent."

Not only that, but when men get back to doing what they know how to do, they regain a sense of competence they may not have at home at first. "My husband intended to take off a week or two and then work half days for another week," says

Stacy. "But after a couple of days he was back working half days. Within a week, he was back full-time. Before the birth, he didn't even want my mother to come, because he wanted to be an involved dad right from the start.

"Yet after the baby was born, he couldn't wait to head back to the office," she says. "He'll tell you it's because it was a critical time at work. But I have to ask, when is it not a critical time where he works? I think his going back to work had more to do with the internal desire to do work that he knew how to do, felt confident doing and a desire to return to some normalcy."

This urge to feel competent, to get back to a world that is orderly and where people actually tell you that you're doing a good job, where you get concrete things done, is something that many women understand, now that most of us work. You may even come to feel it yourself. It was something Lucy understood, and it gave her empathy for her husband in those early days. "I love my work. I love being in my lab. When my leave ended at nine weeks, I was really ready to get back to work, at least part-time."

All this is to say that there are likely to be some shocks in the early days of your post-baby marriage. It may be the sudden disappearing act that your husband pulls. Or the one that you pull, without even realizing it, as you are swallowed up in the haze of baby care, nursing, diaper changes. All you want to do is sleep, and all your husband wants to know is 'What happened to my wife?'

"Kids cause a lot of stress and hardship on a couple," says my friend Beth.

And I say, hold that thought. Underline it. Remember it. The studies verify it. After the first child, couples experience about eight times as much conflict as they did before, according to John Gottman, a psychologist at the University of

Washington who is one of the nation's leading experts on marriage. In fact, the first year after a baby is born is well known among therapists and counselors to be one of the most stressful a couple will ever have to weather. Two thirds of all married people, in fact, suffer a "precipitous drop" in marital satisfaction that year, according to Gottman.

"I always laugh when someone tells me they had children to make their marriage closer," Beth adds. "Especially when you think about what it's like at first. For starters, you're not awake most of the time. And when *you* are, *your husband* is probably sleeping. Somebody's got to sleep! Now, that makes it hard for a relationship to work."

Which brings up the "Who's going to get up this time?" question. Or the "why did you wake her up, when I just got her to sleep" question. Or the "Why are you waking me up, when *you're already up*?" inquiry. These are the leading edge of the questions that follow later, about whose job is more important, who's going to stay home when the baby is sick, and who's going to the pediatrician.

Then there's the other line of questioning, one that arrives just as you are trying to remember what your pre-baby body might have felt like. Just when your most fervent wish might be to find a way to sit down or go to the bathroom without pain. It's the "Are we ever going to have sex again?" question.

Okay. I'll answer that one.

The answer to that last question is yes, even though you may not believe it the first week or two at home. Or even the third week. For most couples, sex does retreat to the back burner during maternity leave. But not forever.

And the good news is that while there is stress aplenty for most couples during maternity leave, there are the other moments that redeem the difficulties of this early time together with the baby, the moments that make the bond between you and your husband deeper and stronger as you barrel through these early weeks. Those moments arrive unexpectedly, when you're admiring the baby together, in awe of her tiny fingers, her perfect little belly, her soft skin. Or when you see your husband do something utterly tender, stroking the baby's head, rubbing her back. You melt, and you feel attracted to him, just as you did in the early days of your romance.

Or the times when he senses how tired you are, and massages your shoulders or strokes your head, or just lets you bawl your eyes out because you are overwhelmed and he senses that's what you need. Or he brings you exactly the right thing to pick up your spirits. For one friend of mine, it was fresh peach milkshakes from a local deli. "I had a craving the first week after my daughter was born, almost like people describe in pregnancy. It was summer and it was hot and I was shaky from the really extreme effort of childbirth. I wanted a milkshake, a peach milkshake. I don't know why. I don't even remember whether I used to have them as a kid or what. But suddenly that was exactly what I wanted. Pat was tired and cranky himself, but every day while I was in the hospital, he went out in the sticky, humid heat and stood on line and got me one. I can still remember the taste of them," she says. "I was touched by that, that he did that for me."

Keeping those memories in mind can be sustaining as you struggle through the first weeks of maternity leave, both of you trying to decide what it means to be a parent, for better or worse. I remind you of this, as if I were your best friend, because most of the time you won't have the presence of mind to remind yourself. Instead, life is likely to overtake you, even as you make some of the most crucial decisions about home and work, decisions that will begin to shape your relationship for years to come.

Like who will stay home with the baby at first? Who will continue to work without interruption?

Whose Job Is This, Anyway?

You've read about stay-at-home dads, real dads who quit their jobs and stay home with the babies. "When people ask me what I did for child care," says one friend. "I tell them I married him."

But most likely you're not married to one. At least that's what the statistics show. Hardly any men—less than 10 percent of new fathers—take paternity leave. This is a fact of life even though the Family and Medical Leave Act gives men the right—the same right that women have—to be home for up to twelve weeks after the baby is born.

There are good reasons why men don't take leaves, even if they *want* to, even if they feel comfortable with babies and want to be there. Money is the main one. It's practically impossible for a man to collect a paycheck while he's home with a newborn. Unlike women, men have no right to disability pay, since they are not disabled by childbirth. Nor can they use their sick time, since they aren't sick. They may have some vacation time coming, but on average, most have only about two weeks a year. And couples often decide they'd rather save that time for a real family vacation. That leaves the handful of companies in this country who offer paid paternity leave. And even those firms tend to be incredibly stingy. A day or two is considered generous.

Given a paycheck, more men would certainly stay home. There's good evidence for that. When Lotus Development

Corporation offered men a full eight weeks of paid leave to care for a new baby, scores of them took the full time off.

Lotus also added another ingredient that helped, an element that research and management consultants say is critical to changing workaholic cultures into father-friendly ones: visible support for that policy. A high-tech employer with new-age ideas, the company made it clear, through publicity in the company's in-house newsletter and contact with the community at large, that it truly wanted new fathers to take the time right alongside their wives. Lotus officials even sought out the national media to get them to do stories about fathers from the company who took full advantage of the policy. That went a long way toward sending a clear message to men that it was okay to take the time.

Of course, I don't need to tell you such attitudes among managers are incredibly rare. Most employers still promote the guy or gal who pretends not to have children at all—even if he or she has five of them. Some even like it when the execs have few friends outside the company and even ignore their spouses—all the more time to focus on work! That makes it tough to for a guy to tell the boss he wants to spend a week or two at home with a new baby. "My husband took a day or two off for each child, but that was it. Even now with the FMLA, he feels that dads cannot take leave for the birth of a child without professional consequences," says Janet, whose husband is a middle manager at a large corporation. Like many working women, Janet tried to cheerlead her husband into leading the charge against such archaic attitudes. "I keep telling him that things would change if some dads would just do it. But he does not want to be a pioneer in this area."

Given these constraints, it's likely you'll be the only parent home for most of the leave. "We could barely afford to think about me taking six weeks off, let alone contemplate losing Jeff's paycheck. I honestly think he might have been better with the baby, but there was no question who was going to be home. I'd get a disability check, and he'd get zip. So I was home," says Terry, a secretary in Maryland.

That's not to say your husband won't be a loving father and bond with the baby in his own way, at his own pace. Some men I know do the night feedings, diapers, baths, the works. They rush home from work to be with that new baby. But most of my friends describe their hubbies as a "big help" in the beginning, and less help as life moves along. And that's something to think about.

Most of the research on working couples shows that it can be valuable to start thinking, right from the start of your maternity leave, about how these early days will begin to shape your new roles—will play out and become reinforced in the future. What does it mean to "help" and what does it mean to "share" and how will that difference change your marriage?

For example, if you stay home now and take a pay cut, your salary will begin to fall behind his, even if the two of you had been earning about the same before. If you decide to go part-time, that situation will only be amplified. As the disparity in your paycheck grows, you, not your husband, will be expected to take the hits at work when there are conflicts between work commitments and your child's needs.

In addition, if you do the lioness's share of the child care, you'll be the one who feels the most adept with the baby, and become the primary parent. And with little hands-on experience, your husband may feel less and less competent with the baby. After a while he may do little except roughhousing with the children when he comes home in the evening.

In fact, hundreds of little adjustments that start in the early days can end up nudging you toward traditional roles, even if you hadn't intended for things to turn out that way. "I figured I should be the one to get up and do the night feedings while I was on leave, since he was the one who had to get up and go to work," says Kristin. But much to her chagrin, once the pattern was set, "it didn't change when I went back to work. I was still the one getting up at night." She was "too tired to fight about it, so I just kept doing it."

It is important to raise these issues because so many women have wound up in what *Parenting* magazine dubs the 70/30 marriage: Mom is still doing 70 percent of the child care and chores and Dad doing 30 percent—even when Mom works full-time. My friends didn't expect things to turn out that way.

Fifty-Fifty Adds Up to a Win

Most of us aspire to a more equal partnership, both at work and at home. And the fact that more of us are going back to work after the baby is born is certainly pushing things in that direction. That 30 percent of child care and housework that men do these days is up from just 10 percent two decades ago. "There's no doubt that men are doing more, and it's because women are working," says Faye Crosby, a professor of psychology at the University of California, Santa Cruz, who has studied women's changing roles. "There's just less resistance among men, more recognition that this is fair."

"Peer marriage" is a term used to describe the kind of marriage where a man and a woman have the same status at work and at home. And studies show that's a good thing for

everybody. Peer marriage is the happiest kind, declares Pep-
per Schwartz, a sociologist who has devoted her career to
peering into the most intimate corners of married people's
lives. Men and women in such marriages share more and so
tend to have more common ground, more empathy, and
more sources of satisfaction in their lives than couples who
choose the old-fashioned model where the father is the
breadwinner and the mother is the housewife. That doesn't
mean you both have to be clawing your way up the corporate ladder. It isn't the content of the jobs, or the level of
success. Rather, it's the fact that you are both walking around
in similar shoes, juggling duties at work and at home.

Janice Steil, a psychologist at Adelphi University who has
also spent years investigating the ingredients of marital bliss,
concurs. Her latest studies are even more intriguing to me
since they probe how the balance of power in marriage affects intimacy. If they don't earn a paycheck—one that's
nearly equal to their husband's—many women simply don't
feel safe enough to disclose feelings that might upset or challenge their mates. The inequality erodes their sense of power
and entitlement. In other words, it's hard to get mad at the
guy who's making the mortgage and car payments. Not that
we like to think too hard about this. "Most women don't like
to think about the issues of power in their most intimate relationships, but a paycheck really does contribute to the way
women feel in their marriages," says Steil. "If they are earning enough, they feel they have the right to speak up and say
how they feel. If not, they may grow more passive, and be
less direct about the things that are bothering them. Women
may start to behave more passively, or to withdraw or to get
resentful." Certainly, the intimacy in the marriage erodes.
"Intimacy is all about revealing yourself, about being able to

be yourself, sharing your true feelings. Without that ability, marriage really changes."

I'm not saying that there is a rule and you have to be totally fifty-fifty about everything or else. If that were the case, most modern marriages would collapse right now. But fifty-fifty is a nifty goal to set. Thinking about this goal means that you are both doing your best to create an atmosphere of reciprocity and mutual respect. Without that, most any relationship will founder, even marriage to the man you love most.

After all, most of us just don't have the energy or patience to keep doing two thirds of the child care and household chores after putting in a full day on the job. That's why I'm suggesting that you give some attention to these issues and start laying down some positive rules and goals right at the beginning, before your maternity leave starts.

Getting to Fifty-Fifty

So how do you get from him "helping" to him truly sharing the care?

With some real effort, that's how.

Sorry, girls, there just doesn't appear to be any other way.

No matter what nice guys we married, you're both going to be pulled toward an unequal marriage if you don't watch it. It just happens, as you adjust to all those details of life that are set up to accommodate the old-fashioned breadwinner dad, homemaker mom model. Like the fact he can't even get a decent leave to start with. After that, it's the hours at work, the fact that men are viewed less kindly than women when they talk about work/family conflicts on the job, the fact that so many people expect you to be primary caregiver, even the child-care center, after you get back to work. "We left Mike's number with the day care, and explained he's the one to call when Chelsea gets sick," says Rebecca. "He's the one with the flexible schedule. I can barely get up out of my seat at work to go to the ladies' room. But it never fails. They still call me first, and I have to call Mike."

Be aware that you may even feed into this stuff at first. Even if you're currently nodding your head that it really would be in your best interests not to be the one slaving away at midnight, doing the dishes or mopping the floor while your husband's asleep in bed. Even if you believe that you might really resent your mate somewhere down the road if that's the way things turn out.

That's because these beliefs may be what you *think,* but not exactly what you *feel* at the start.

What you may feel in the early days is a surprising and deep attachment to that baby, and a desire to be that baby's *primary* parent. Or what we used to just call, back in the bad old days, Mom. In fact, you might even feel a little insecure and guilty when Dad takes the baby and changes a diaper and it all goes just a little too smoothly. Like the baby doesn't need you as much as you thought she did.

Sure, it's a great *idea* to have Dad involved. But aren't babies supposed to prefer their moms? "I was really upset when Tyler reached out his arms and actually cried out to go to Michael," says Elisabeth. "I didn't want to feel that way. It surprised me. But there it was. I just felt inadequate. I mean, I just kept thinking, maybe I'm a bad mother. Isn't the baby supposed to prefer *me*?"

Besides, you're not sure your husband knows what he's doing. Especially if he's not sure he knows what he's doing. No matter that you still don't feel like you know what you're doing. That's different. You're the mom. You'll learn. And within a week of being home, everyone is deferring to you anyway. Like you really do know what you are doing.

So it's okay if everyone applauds Dad for pitching in occasionally. But when he really tries to be an equal parent, or proves that he really can be one, you may have to fight off some strong feelings. "I guess I just felt displaced. Or maybe it was replaced. Or jealous," says Elisabeth. "I'm not even sure. I just know it was powerful."

Indeed. It's another one of those little nuggets of wisdom tucked away in the literature on changing families. At root, the way families are changing is really challenging some of our heart-felt beliefs about what it means to be a man or a woman, a mother or a father. Violating the rules of gender can set off alarms so deep in your psyche that you didn't even know you had them. It can show up in the most ridiculous ways as well. A friend of mine in Texas, a high-powered corporate gal, ran home every night to sit with her seven-year-old daughter for piano practice and then to cook lavish gourmet meals for her daughter and husband. Since her husband was a professor with a flexible schedule, perfectly willing to do both the piano practice and prepare dinner, she knew she was being irrational. It took her a while to figure that out. "I think I was trying to prove I was a real woman," she says. Fortunately, once she identified the feeling, she could let go of it, and let her hubby do the cooking. Or even buy takeout every once in a while.

This is another one of those little pieces of information I share in hopes that you'll store it away for use when you find yourself having such feelings. So you'll be prepared to deal with feelings that can really define your relationship for so many years. So you can ignore them. That's where all the effort comes in. So you can remember you're a perfectly good mother, even when you share the care. His good behavior is not a minus for you. It's a plus for your kids, your relationship, and you. It's a way to escape raccoon eyes, if nothing else!

The couples I know who successfully buck the temptation to fall into traditional roles understand that. That's why they make a conscious and deep commitment to equality in their marriage, right from the start. Sometimes even before the baby arrives. "My husband and I made a decision way before we had children that when we did, one of us would stay home full-time for as long as possible," says Jenny. "Since I made more money and had a better career future, it made sense for me to go back to work and for him to stay home. Which is what we did. The baby was born in October, and I took six weeks off. Then he quit his job the week before Thanksgiving, and we had a week home together before I went back to work."

Even then, she concedes, life was not without its bumps. In fact, she says, "The first six to eight months were rough as he learned the ropes."

Jenny is not the only woman to observe that such a complete role reversal can test your mettle, and your mate's. "One day my husband called me up and told me he had an emergency," she said, laughing. "When I asked him what the emergency was, he told me he had an 'extreme diaper' to deal with. I told him I thought he could deal with that. And he did."

"But another time, he actually brought the baby in to me in the office, in a stroller, and left her. He just said he'd had enough. It took us some talking to get to the other side of that one." But get through it they did, she says, adding that there's a real reward in the end. "Now the kids will turn to him as much as to me. They have two parents they can totally rely on."

Another couple I know took a different path toward equal parenting, one that more parents are trying out. They both took a leave, one after the other. "My husband had paid paternity leave, so we agreed that we'd take sequential leaves," says Maryann. It did not happen without glitches. "The night before he came on board we were worried because our daughter was refusing a bottle. I was pumping like a fiend and nervous." The next day, when Maryann called at noon to see how things were going, "Of course, she was drinking rather than starving."

The payoff for this kind of struggle? A mutual appreciation of what it takes to both care for a baby and earn a living—and therefore a mutual appreciation of and respect for each other. "I had to be the breadwinner for a while when Don lost his job," says one mom. "Up until then, I'd somehow thought of my job as optional. It wasn't really, but I thought of it like that. And Don felt the burden of earning the higher income, of being the provider. I don't think I really understood that until I had to walk a mile in his shoes."

Not only that, but after being at home, Don became a more confident parent. "Don learned to trust his instincts and not defer to mine," she says. These days, they both work full-time and share the care at home. And she feels content. "We really understand and appreciate each other more now."

Ditto says Sarah, a publicist whose husband is a salesman. "We have a true split of responsibilities and I can't imagine what mothers go through who do not," she says. It started on her maternity leave, even though he never stayed home. Every other night, he got up for the night feedings, even though he had to go to work the next morning. "He understood that I'd be exhausted if I did it all the time, and he wanted to have a real relationship with the kids, right from the start. I can't imagine how I'd feel if I thought I had to do all the child care, plus maintain a job and a household. I have a gem of a spouse. I know that and I love him for it."

Another woman tells me that she and her spouse adopted a simple arrangement while she was still on leave. "Our agreement was that whoever was the POD—Parent On Deck—did what they thought was appropriate without criticism."

Such an agreement will serve you well, even if you aren't always that generous. There's sure to be tension, even bickering, when it comes to all those unsavory household chores, like cleaning the toilets or wiping up baby spit-up in the middle of the night. But sharing the care now will most certainly save you more tension later, when both of you are asking: Who will drop the baby off at day care? Pick up the baby? Pick up the groceries? Pick up the house?

Staying Close: Sex After Baby

Oh, yes, then there's that other part of marriage, the sexual connection. The affection and the love. Leisurely and delicious. Some wonderful rituals and playful moments. Tender and sweet or passionate and piercing, it kept you and your mate close.

Now the idea seems remote.

Sex?

The first week, I felt like a cross between a beached whale and a war victim. Or maybe a refugee from a major earthquake. Childbirth, after all, is something that happens to your body. No matter how wonderful the result, the process is a physical trauma, with wrenching pain, followed by raging hormones. Which is why the doctors give us those six to eight weeks to recover. And when you wake up, your life has changed. Now there're three of you in the house all the time, and one of you is incredibly needy. A baby about it, in fact.

So it's not surprising that parenting magazines run all those articles titled something like "Is There Sex After the Baby?" Though I must admit that even asking the question at first seemed to me rather sadistic on the editors' part. There I was lying in bed with a scar from a cesarean, and a nurse was telling me the very first day that I was going to get up and walk down the hall that day. I had serious questions about her sanity. And kindness. Maybe she, too, was sadistic.

Well, I did the walking. But I didn't enjoy that day and I couldn't imagine that I was going to enjoy it any time soon.

After the second birth, a vaginal delivery, sitting was the problem. There was the episiotomy. And do I dare tell you I also had hemorrhoids? Embarrassing but true, and I learned only after that delivery that it's quite a common thing with vaginal deliveries. Everything healed and went away. But it took a full six weeks before I could sit down without thinking about it.

In addition, I was still carting around those extra twenty pounds that all the medical authorities had told me not to gain. And I told myself not to gain. But gain I had, and they took about six months to disappear.

Sex?

I checked in with a couple friends, wondering how long it took for them to get interested in the idea again. "Oh, weeks and weeks. Or maybe months after the first. I can't even re-member now," says Frieda. "But I do remember how I felt then. It was not just giving birth. It was also the nursing. Nursing was such a demand, a physical demand. I remember I felt like I had that baby hanging on my body all day long. When he did take a break, I didn't want to be touched. I wanted to be left alone. I wanted my body back."

Indeed.

The trauma of birth is most certainly something that happens only to you, not to your mate, and even if your man was there in the delivery room, it may be hard for him to empathize with how you feel afterward. Like you were hit by a truck, mostly. Happy, maybe. Or shaky. But definitely as if you'd been beaten up or hit by a large truck.

And then there are the changes in your breasts, whether you end up nursing or not. Your milk comes in, you're probably engorged for a while and experience some tenderness, especially if you decide not to breastfeed. If you do nurse, there's that new demand on your body, one that exhausts many women for a while. And there is often vaginal dryness that accompanies breastfeeding, at least in the beginning.

In addition, there can be loads of other feelings, as hormones adjust to our nonpregnant, postpartum selves. Hot flashes, sweating, anxiety, mood swings. Weeping for no apparent reason.

And we're tired.

Sex?

Well, all of it does pass. But not even as quickly as many babies begin to settle, which is at three weeks. More likely, your body will need the full six to eight weeks to recover and feel comfortable again. For some women, especially those who have had a cesarean, it takes much longer to recuperate; the skin around the incision may be tender for even up to six months if weight or pressure is put on the wrong spot.

But even after we're healed, most of us are still tired, in emotional upheaval, and more attuned to the needs of the demanding new being in our lives than to our sexual needs or those of our mate. "I was always on edge, even when the baby was asleep. I figured he was going to wake up any minute. And for a while, that really happened. He was very demanding and very unpredictable."

So it is true that sex takes a nosedive for months after the baby is born. Even a year. Which is exactly what most of the moms I know came to accept as a natural state for a while.

Still, your husband may not appreciate this. Once he sees that you are sitting, walking, and talking more normally, he may want to be intimate again. He may miss you, after such a long hiatus. He may want to be reassured, feel close again, now that the baby is there and so many things have changed. "After a few weeks, Ted began to talk about sex," said Frieda. "He really missed it. I tried not to just push him away, but I'd be thinking, 'Are you kidding? Get out of here! You must be kidding! I might be walking but I'm not ready for anyone to touch me yet!' I don't think men can understand what is going on at first."

Indeed, it's almost a cliché among therapists that many men often feel ignored and unattended once the baby arrives, especially if you are nursing. "I just had no desire. I didn't like that things were that way," says Beth. "In fact, I felt sorry for Richard. We'd had a very good sex life before Andrew was born. But for months afterward, I had no interest. None."

Her solution? "I just tried to explain it to him. I tried to explain how worn out I was, how tired I was from all of the physical demands of pregnancy and then childbirth and nursing," she says. The main thing that helped, she adds, is that she made it clear that she was not rejecting him, just putting things on hold for a while. "I told him how much I still loved him, and that I saw this baby as evidence of that deep love. But I needed to recover before I could even think about sex." She also began to do more hugging and cuddling in bed, just staying close.

As far as I can tell, Beth intuitively followed every bit of the good advice that comes from the hordes of psychologists and counselors who deal with couples adjusting to the situation. Like Lucy, she has a lot of affection and empathy for her spouse and that helped see them through.

I've also had friends confide in me that their men got angry, withdrew, or just distanced themselves. Some of those soothing words that Beth used might have helped, I would guess. Or maybe it just takes time for everyone to get used to the new realities of family life. None of my friends, even the ones who had some sparks fly, ever experienced a serious rift in the long run because of the lack of sex in the early months after the baby. For most, things were getting back on track at around six months or so.

Other friends say sex was just a nonevent and a nonissue for a while. "We were both so tired, I think sex just dropped off the radar screen," says one.

And so it goes for many of us. One survey found that three fourths of new parents reported a dramatic drop in the frequency of sexual relations, with exhaustion given as the main reason. "I don't think either of us had any interest for nearly two months after Jake's birth," says one mom. "And then it was less frequent. But good, it got better and better."

You never really know what's what in other people's bedrooms, no matter what your friends tell you. But if most of my friends are honest on this point, and the research is accurate, it's wise to assume that there isn't much desire or much time for much sex on maternity leave, especially the first time around. "It's not like we even talked about it at all. There was so much else going on. It's more like we were in a tunnel with the baby, unable to see outside of life with her. I think we both knew that we still loved each other, and we felt close, but sex just wasn't part of it, not for a while," says Kristin.

As my daughter would say, "Well, duh." Finding the energy, the time, and the focus for sex after the birth of a baby is difficult in the early months. But life settles, and most couples are sane enough to anticipate that as well. As Susie says, "I just assumed, yes, we'd have sex after the baby. Of course, we would. But not right after the baby. Maybe not even for weeks or months after the baby. But it was kind of like we were oblivious. We slept together, we slept with the baby, we were close. We were even blissful at times."

And for Susie, sex now is better than it used to be. "Having this baby together, and seeing Bob with the baby has made us so much closer. Sure, there are times when we're tired and fed up with each other. We've had some really bad fights. But on balance, the experience of having this child has just made us closer. I know it sounds a little sappy, but I look at her sometimes, and I see Bob in her and I am reminded that she is the product of our love, our connection. And that makes me feel good. And feeling good, feeling close to Bob, makes sex better."

Chapter 7

When the Boss Calls
and the Baby's Crying

*K*ate is a senior executive at a dot.com in San Francisco that is actually still in business. In fact, it's thriving, after a brief round of layoffs. And so are Kate and her new baby, even though she signed on to work during her entire three-month maternity leave. As one of the key players in the company, she couldn't figure out any other way to hang on to her job. She loves her work, and was ecstatic to learn she was pregnant, so she just winged it, keeping in touch by phone, fax, and e-mail.

The arrangement had its hairy moments. "Okay, I admit, it was not the perfect way to do maternity leave," she says. "When the guys call and the baby's crying, you have to decide who to put on hold."

Mostly, it was the guys, she admits. Babies have a way of insisting on attention, in a far more compelling way than even the most cantankerous board member. And mostly, the guys took Kate's situation in stride. She works for one of those new-age companies where the guys in charge are mostly forty and under, have working wives, and often insist they'd really like to be home with their babies themselves. And they all work in San Francisco, for God's sake, one of the nation's hippest cities. It would have been very uncool to be anything but "family-friendly" to Kate while she was caring for her new baby.

Still, there was one thing Kate could have used during her leave. In fact, after talking with Kate, I am ready to say it is an essential tool for all new moms who plan to take calls from the office while on leave. Especially conference calls with your entire board of directors. That tool is a phone with a mute button, so no one can hear what the heck is going on at your end of the line. It takes exactly one anecdote from Kate to convert me to this idea. "How about the time I was nursing during a conference call from the board and I had to apologize for the loud, enthusiastic moans my daughter made while thoroughly enjoying her meal?" Kate asks me. Somehow, those new-age guys weren't embarrassed, nor was Kate. She is one of the most confident women I know. "I explained it, we had a giggle, and then ignored it and went on to have a great board meeting."

I still keep trying to picture that. The relaxed giggle of male coworkers at the sound of the nursing baby. I get hives just thinking about the reactions I'd have gotten from some of my male bosses to that exact same call. They would have had hives, as well. Or at least a passing rash and would have hemmed and hawed enough to derail any serious business conversation. I don't want to even think about what they might have said to each other after they hung up. All I can ever say to Kate is that she seems to inhabit a different planet than I do. She shares the same universe as Diane Keaton, who, in that old movie *Baby Boom*, was able to make serious headway in the business world with baby in tow.

In the meantime, most of my other friends shared the same fervent hope that I did about contact with the office during maternity leave, at least in the first few weeks.

We all wished there'd be none.

That is, if and when we thought about the office at all. In most cases, life with the new baby swept in like a tidal wave, temporarily swamping us. "Office? What office," joked my friend Beth on her fifth day home. "I'm just trying to get dressed today. If I'm lucky, I might do it."

Even by the time we could finally get dressed on the very same day we got out of bed, work dropped to the bottom of the priority list for a while. Or even longer, in some cases. "My only goal on maternity leave was to enjoy my baby," says Sheri. "I knew things were changing at work. I had a new boss, new people coming in all around me, and I knew I should be at least a little worried about work. I was always conscientious and I cared a lot about doing a professional job. But to tell you the truth, I just didn't want to think about it after the baby was born. I just wanted to enjoy my baby."

For my money, Sheri has her eyes on the right prize. Nothing will ever replace that time at home with your baby. Still, she was more ostrichlike than most of my friends, maybe even a little too head-in-the-sand by my lights, totally ignoring work at a time of critical change. With a new boss and a restructuring of her department under way, she could easily have faced a difficult future when she returned to work. Or no future at all.

The reality is that as precious as the time is, you still need to work. You have to feed that baby—more than breastmilk, in the long run. And buy him clothes. Pay the mortgage. Details like that. So it's a good idea to figure out the best strategy for keeping in touch with your workplace while you're out on leave.

In fact, when you look back, you may even realize that maternity leave turned out to be the first challenge, an audition for your new act as working mom. Happily, most of us don't have to choreograph board meetings via conference call as Kate did. Nor do too many of us have to deal with a brand-new boss showing up a few weeks before we go out on leave, as Sheri did.

But we still have to figure out, for the first time, how we will fit everything in our new lives into a single day. What *will* you do when the baby's crying and the boss is calling? How many calls do you want to receive from the office once you're home? How many will you *have* to take, even if you don't want to? Is it okay to miss a meeting with the head of your department? Can you get any work done with a baby in your lap? These are just the first of many questions you'll face as you learn to juggle work and a baby. They are part of the push/pull that comes with the territory.

You'll figure it all out, over time. In fact, you'll probably discover yourself to be that incredibly adaptive and flexible variety of the human species, a mom who works. You'll find life more fluid than you ever dreamed, sometimes challenging your patience and resourcefulness. Yet, you'll learn to go with the flow, setting your priorities to suit what's happening at home and at work. Just as Kate did. She kept right on working because she knew that job was a once-in-a-lifetime opportunity and she and her baby would do just fine. Just as Sheri did. She'd waited a long time for her baby. Now in her second, and this time happy, marriage, she didn't want to give up one minute with her new child. She knew she could get another equally good job in her field if she had to. So she put the job on a back burner for a while. Both women are happy with the path they chose.

It almost sounds simple, when you look at it from the outside.

But coming out of the gate right after the baby is born, all those decisions about how and when and why to keep in touch with your boss and coworkers can be more than a little confusing. You may even be something of a nut case in the first few weeks, bawling one moment and euphoric the next. How can you work and raise a kid, you ask yourself. Maybe you should just quit.

And that's just how you're feeling as you step into the much-longed-for shower, turn on the water, get soaking wet, only to hear the phone ringing, which wakes the baby. Fool that you are, and acting on automatic pilot, you answer said phone, only to discover your boss's deputy on the other end of the line, one of your most methodical, slow-talking, can't-see-the-forest-for-the-trees kind of people, asking you an inconsequential question.

One that he could easily have asked someone else in the office, if only he'd thought of it. Almost anyone else in the office, in fact.

At that moment, all you want to do is throw in the towel, both literally and figuratively.

It's the Job, Stupid

Put that thought on hold. Stop answering the phone. What you need at the start of your maternity leave is an answering machine, voice mail, any trusty little technology that takes these calls without becoming irate. Your mother or sister might suffice.

And remind yourself first and foremost why you're keeping in touch. You need the job, remember? Or some job, and this is the one you happen to have right now.

So try to make the best of it. Some of us did have to take some calls from the office, even very early on, and learn to deal with those folks on the other end with some professional aplomb. In the long run, it will be in your interest not to lose all contact with folks at work. Before you know it, you will be back in shape and back at the job, working closely with them. And even if you wind up switching jobs, you'll still need their goodwill. These are the same people who are going to write your next job recommendation.

So try to get things a little under control, and think about the messages that you are sending back to work. And try to bear in mind that the first thing that everyone back on the job wants from you right now is reassurance.

That's right, *they* want to be reassured, even though *you're* the one who just had the baby.

They all want to know, for sure, that you are coming back and that you still care about your job. Whether you work on the assembly line, clean hotel rooms, or run a corporate marketing department, they all want to know that you still want this job and to be with this company. Did I say this before? Did I say this one hundred times before? Well, maybe five. But that's because it's so critical.

Above all, your boss wants to be reassured. No matter that you set your return date in stone and pledged your first-born as collateral for every promise that you made. Now you are out, and he went out on a limb, getting you that extra pay, part-time return, or extra time off. Now he wants to be certain that you're going to uphold your end of the bargain.

Or you may have one of those bosses, male or female, who believes, deep-down, that no woman comes back after a baby. No matter that every new mom except one has come back within six weeks for the past two hundred years because every new mom needed the paycheck. What this boss remembers is the one who didn't.

Or your supervisor may be genuinely empathetic to your plight. With children of his own and a wife who works, he may know firsthand how hard it is to figure out all the logistics and make it back to work. Or your boss may be a she, one who has struggled with her own decisions about how to balance work and family.

Whatever drives your boss's current anxiety, you need to address it. That's why your first and most important way of keeping in touch is simply to reassure everybody. You can do it by phoning in during one of those rare, lucid moments when you're awake and someone else can tend the baby. And you can do it even when you foolishly take a call that you should have sent to voice mail.

Even that slow-talking deputy to the boss who's on the phone right now. Try to call up that state of mind you used when you met with your boss about your proposal for maternity leave. Be as confident, self-possessed, and matter-of-fact as you can be. Get rid of the ambivalence, dispense with the complaints or irritation. Save those for your friends outside the workplace. For the moment, you want the entire office to believe that you can't wait to get started again.

That's the main way to hang on to your reputation as a serious, dedicated worker. And this will be your challenge for the next, oh, twenty-one years of your life, when coworkers and bosses find out you have a child at home. Everyone knows that most babies are a lot more engaging and demanding and call up more loyalty than most jobs. And now that you've laid eyes on your very own, they can't help but worry that you won't give work the same priority, that you won't care as much, won't go the extra mile. That you won't be a team player. And that they'll have to pick up the slack. From now on, they wonder, will your family come first?

Of course it will. But that doesn't mean you'll be a bad worker. In fact, many of the moms I know are the best workers, more efficient and more focused in the time that they're on the job. But many bosses don't see things that way. They see family as a conflict, a sign of your divided loyalties. In fact, you've already put your family first by taking time off to start one. For the worst bosses, this is treason. Will you be sloppy and distracted? Miss days and days of work when the baby's sick? Like to look at *Parenting* magazine more than the company newsletter?

In a more humane culture, indeed, in most other industrialized countries in the world, your behavior would be seen in a more grown-up way. Instead of treason, most employers are required by law to treat having children as a natural right of passage for most adults. After all, most grown-ups do wind up having children and also have to earn the money to house, feed, and clothe them. That's why most other countries offer women a paid leave, free or low-cost health benefits, and even a family allowance to buffer new expenses. In some countries, you'd even have the legal right to work part-time until your child started school. And the right to take up to six weeks paid vacation a year, in recognition of the fact that families need time off work and time together.

These other countries have already recognized that our babies grow up to be future workers and citizens, the ones who keep everything going when we get too old, weak, and tired out to do it anymore. It only makes sense to make sure these kids get off to a good start, which means giving working parents the support they need to make a living while they're raising their kids.

But of course, we live in the United States, where most employers still struggle to accept these facts of life. About a half dozen have truly family-friendly policies, but generally, having a baby is still seen as the ultimate conflict with work, something that will rob you of your ability to focus on work. Certainly, that's the message behind most policies on the job, and as a consequence, the way most bosses still see your situation. Now that you've had the baby, what comes next? Will you push back your return date? Decide to quit altogether? Start to miss work when the baby's sick? Turn into a slacker?

So you need to put those questions to rest. Even if you think you may want to slow down eventually, now is not the time to start that conversation. Right now, while on maternity leave, you want to hang on to your title of serious worker. A worker with a future. A team player.

That idea can seem distant as you hold that sleeping baby's head to your cheek. But if you concentrate for a minute and pull up some memories of how things work at work, you'll see my point.

First of all, the not-so-serious workers are the ones who never get off the assembly line, languish in back offices, and never get a chance to be a manager or a supervisor. Raises are puny, or they don't materialize at all. And even worse, you may be passed over for a promotion that could actually simplify your life—get you more money, better hours, more control over your time, more opportunities in your career when your kids are older. And when things get tight, and layoffs are imminent, you'll be first in line for the pink slip.

Whether you consider yourself ambitious or not, it pays to think about these consequences for the way you present yourself on leave. Even Stephanie, an office manager, who talks nonstop about how Regis may someday make her a millionaire, if only she could just get on his show, has come to terms with how to work smart. "I made sure to keep in touch with my boss while I was out on leave. Nothing really big, just checking in and letting him know I was still on the planet. I did not really want to work after I had kids. But I don't have a choice about it," she says. "And since I didn't have a choice about it, I wanted my time away from the baby to be worth it. I wanted to enjoy my job as much as I could. I wanted to make as much money as I possibly could. And I do."

There are other reasons to stay in touch. Especially with the reliable gossips. Not the rumor mongers who breathlessly and indiscriminately pass along the stuff that never materializes or isn't important. But the ones who have their ear to the ground, and tend to know stuff ahead of everyone else. Remember, bosses change, companies get bought and sold, departments reorganize. Stuff happens, stuff that can dramatically change your position while you're out on leave. And it may be news that your boss won't share with you until it suits him, even though it could affect you. "My boss left the company, and I found a project that I was coming back to lead was going to be cut," says Martha, a marketing executive with a financial services company. "I was lucky that the company had a strong policy of trying to place people elsewhere, but of course the question was, where would that be? I was able to keep up on things by talking a lot with my colleagues. I stayed in touch, just to find out what was going on, and also to remind them that I wanted to be reassigned to a good project."

Finally, consider keeping in touch to be part of your personal disaster-prevention program. Sure, you wrote out a plan for how your work is getting done while you're out. But is it working? "I had left my boss a plan, and he agreed to it," says Peggy, who works in accounts payable of a publishing house. "But a month into my leave, I checked my voice mail and found it was full with people calling me about all the invoices that hadn't been sent to accounting. It turned out that the person who was filling in for me had gotten sick for a week and no one was bird-dogging the invoices that came in from vendors and freelance workers. About thirty of them were still sitting on her desk. I never would have found that out if I hadn't been checking in on a regular basis."

Rhonda, an executive secretary, had a similar experience. "I called a few weeks before I was coming back, only to find that the temp had quit and the work was piling up on my desk," she says. "I guess I should have known that could happen. My boss is a very difficult and demanding person to work for, and the temp just decided to take another job."

Armed with that knowledge, Rhonda was able to collaborate with one of her best friends at work to get another temp into the office until she returned. "It could have been a disaster. I could have had three weeks' worth of work on my desk," she says. "Thank god I called in."

Surviving the First Three Weeks

By now you are probably convinced. You know you have to stay in touch. But what about those early days when you know that you'll be comatose, in pain, and just trying to figure out how to nurse that baby?

Good question.

In the first two to three weeks at least, the main thing you want to do is be in charge of all communication, setting the rules for when and how it will happen. Remember, if you pick up the phone and it's someone from work, you can't hang up on them, even though it may be just as annoying as those dinner-time calls from salespeople trying to give you a great deal on Florida swampland. Except this is worse. You've never been this tired before, and your boss or your colleague wants some real information from you. They expect you to *think,* for God's sake. And they may expect you to do that immediately upon arrival home from the hospital.

Leslie, a senior manager at a pharmaceutical company, started getting calls within twelve hours of the birth of her baby. "I was really sleep-deprived, and all I wanted to do was just take care of my baby and myself," she says. "I just wanted the department to run by itself. I was so annoyed with all the calls. I couldn't believe it was happening."

Thus, it pays to think of home sweet home as a bunker of sorts at first, with a perimeter that virtually no one from your office can penetrate without your permission. And keep those defenses in place for at least the first three weeks. Your rule: You never answer an unexpected call. They don't have to know of your newly adopted bunker mentality. You will keep in touch, but you will do it all on your own terms. "Avoidance," Leslie says. "Avoidance is the best policy, the only policy if people start calling right away. Use voice mail, an answering machine, e-mail. Don't answer the phone. Let the machine get it and return calls when you can."

Also, once the machine or voice mail is in place, unplug the phone itself so it doesn't ring. Otherwise, you'll be cursing the callers who wake both you and the baby. Remember, you can call back. You can always call back. It took me six years, all the way until the birth of my second child, to think of this. With Rachel I used the answering machine, but we were still awakened fairly constantly by that ringing phone.

The beauty of this system, besides allowing you to get a few minutes of shut-eye here and there, is that it gives you time to figure out how to respond to the queries coming your way. This is key. If you pick up the phone just any old time, you may find someone asking a complicated or delicate question—or, face it, in the early days, even a simple question—that you can't answer at that moment. Not without sounding a wee bit, shall we say, unprofessional. As in groggy, incoherent, and rambling. So take charge of the calls by screening them.

And take advantage of all that other technology that keeps you in control of when you make human contact with coworkers and colleagues. "E-mail was the best," Leslie says. "I could do e-mail between 10 P.M. and 2 A.M., the only time when I had some peace and quiet, and then my coworkers would get it at their convenience, the next day."

Finally, there's the old-fashioned polite boundary setting that you can do even before you go out on leave. Ask if they can hold off on anything but dire emergencies for a couple of weeks. Suggest the best times for you to take calls, if you can imagine any—like maybe when you have another adult in the house to hold and soothe the baby. Try to get everyone to avoid late afternoons, since they are generally the worst times for babies and moms alike.

In most cases, your coworkers and bosses will respect such ground rules once you set them up. In fact, most people aren't going to want to intrude, unless your absence interferes with *their* ability to do their job. That's where that plan you made for maternity leave comes in. If you've arranged for someone to handle the critical tasks, especially for your first three weeks at home, you're likely to weather the rest.

If you supervise a dozen or more people, needless to say, that phone's going to be ringing nonstop from the moment you get home from the hospital unless you've got a plan to deal with your supervisees' questions.

The best solution is to select a deputy, someone with enough authority to field questions and keep the most pesky people from bothering you. Especially when 90 percent of those problems can be solved without your input. There are two benefits to this strategy. Number one, you get a little peace. Number two, your deputy gets some good on-the-job training. "Before I went out," says Julie, an office manager for a mid-sized company. "I told everyone to pass their concerns along to Rebecca, my assistant, to decide whether it really needed my attention. It was a great opportunity for her, a time when she could learn how to respond to the day-to-day stuff that comes up, and decide how to respond. So she learned a lot."

Smart woman that she is, Julie also gave Rebecca some concrete guidelines for decision-making. "The big one was 'Can it wait?' If the answer was yes, she had to figure out the next question, 'For how long?'" To answer that, she had to think about what the consequences were of just letting it go for a day, a few days, or even a week. A lot of times, the urgency to call me passed once she answered those questions. I dealt with a lot of things in e-mail, which was easier than constant phone calls.

"The other big issue she had to deal with, if the work couldn't wait, was 'Can someone besides Julie deal with this? Who has the knowledge, authority, and expertise?' In a couple of cases, that took me out of the loop altogether for a few days."

Not forever, however. Julie also had her assistant regularly e-mail to her updates on the work that was passed along, so she could follow up if she needed to and make sure it got done.

Thank God most of us don't have such demanding jobs. Or difficult bosses. Most of my friends tell me that their coworkers behaved much as mine did, apologizing for their interruptions and asking right at the outset if they were calling at a good time.

But there are always the horror stories, which is why I suggest you be prepared for the worst. Laurie had a middle-management job for a midwestern company at the time her first child was born, and the folks at that company wasted no time intruding on her during her leave. "Work was calling me at home constantly and dropping things off for me to read. At one point, they even sent two people over from the office to go over some papers. They were just totally bottom-line driven, and not focused on any family or personal issues," she says.

She survived her leave and made it back to work in one piece only because her husband was supportive, and was able take a substantial amount of time off to be home with the baby. But eventually she quit the company and moved on. Her experience further confirmed for me what so many studies by management consultants have shown: Companies that treat working parents especially poorly usually just aren't very good companies to work for in the first place. "All of the research I've seen shows that good employers are just good employers. They treat everyone as grownups they can trust. There is a respect for the workforce that shows up in all their policies," says Ellen Galinksy, president of the Families and Work Institute in New York City. "And employers who treat workers badly in one area also tend to do that across the board."

You probably already know what kind of company you work for, and so that should influence how you keep in touch. If you work in a place like Laurie's company, you'll need more than an answering machine. You'll need to call up every polite and professional ounce of reserve you have, and then start sending out résumés so you can work at a place that is more respectful of its employees.

When No One Calls at All

You may also encounter the opposite problem while you're out on leave. I have friends who say they never heard a peep from their bosses or coworkers, even at the end of a month's time, and they began to feel spooked. "It's not that I was dying to talk to everyone at work, but I began to wonder whether they missed me at all, or whether they were going to decide they could just do without me," says Meredith. "I had to really push them to stay in touch. People were so respectful of my time with my baby that I had to constantly reassure them that it was *okay* to call me at home."

This experience is a fairly common one for anyone who's ever worked at home on a regular basis, at least at first. Since home and work are so distinctly separate for most of us, many coworkers are shy about bothering you there. Of course, that's fine for the first few weeks. And even a few more if you have to get back to the job in six weeks or so. On such a short leave, you need all the rest you can get. Make one or two check-in calls, and then let them leave you alone.

But if you are taking more time off, especially if you are stretching that leave out over three, four, or five months, encourage people to call you. Within a month, you'll be up and around, even if still unfocused. And by the third and fourth month, you'll even be carrying on conversations, that sort of thing. So it's time to start finding out what's happening at work.

And, let me repeat, in case you weren't paying attention, that it does pay to stay in touch. If only to make sure you have a job and a company to return to. You can also begin to lay the groundwork to smooth your reentry. "I was out for four months, and I wished a couple of people had called me more often. There were some details on some reports that I could have helped with, and it would have made things smoother when I came back. As it worked out, there were some mistakes made that I had to clean up after when I came back," says Lucy.

Working from Home

If you've read this far in this book, you know what I think of trying to do serious work on maternity leave.

I don't think it's a very good idea.

But sometimes, it's the only way. The only way to keep your job. The only way to collect a paycheck. Or it turns out to be the most creative way to stretch the time with your baby. Working half-time, for example, might be the best way to stretch the last month of your leave into two and save you the shellshock of returning full-time.

Whatever your reasons for taking this route, your strategies for keeping in touch will be different. For starters, you'll have to stay in touch; it's part of the deal. Even when you don't want to.

Suppose you have agreed to work half-time, starting with the third week of your "leave." How do you manage? With plans that are even better and more detailed than the ones you made for the times when *other* people would be doing your work. Why? Because otherwise you may get swamped with work raining down on you from a boss and coworkers delighted that they won't have to replace you or even think of you as being on leave for an extra minute. "I told them I'd work half-time, but we didn't decide exactly what I'd be do-ing," says Stacy, a graphic designer for an academic pub-

lisher. "So it turned out to be more like time and a half."
Cindy tells a similar tale. "Once I was back on the payroll,
even though it was only half-time, my boss started to have
full-time expectations of me," she says. "I really wished I'd
laid it all out a little more clearly at the beginning. It's hard
to come back to someone afterwards and say, 'I really can't
work that hard or that much.' But I finally did, because I was
going nuts with all the work he was sending my way."

To avoid that fate, set up a clear understanding with your
boss before you set foot outside the office. Lay out exactly
what work you're doing, how many hours you'll be putting
in, and how and when you'll get that work to the office. And
try to establish some times when you know you can take or
return calls.

That way, you'll avoid unrealistic expectations and short
tempers all around. Especially yours. Setting clear expectations has another beneficial effect. Your boss and colleagues
really will know exactly what you're accomplishing at home,
and will appreciate your productivity. "I made sure that my
work was measurable during the time I was home. I pre-
sented a list of tasks so management could see that there
were substantial and doable things to be done from home,"
says Lois, who designs school curriculums for an educa-
tional consulting firm. "Otherwise I have a feeling they'd
picture me just napping or raiding the refrigerator. And I
was working hard."

And once the company sees what you're doing, you may
also be able to get them to foot the bill for the tools you need
to get the work done—a laptop, a phone, a fax, maybe even
an extra phone line. These days, with more and more companies accustomed to having at least some workers telecommuting, it's worth asking. In some states, like Oregon and
California, your firm might even get a tax break for turning

you into a telecommuter. Those states are desperately trying to get commuters off the road, to cut down on air pollution. So they reward employers who help them achieve that goal by offering tax breaks on equipment used in employees' home offices.

Finally, if you plan to do some work at home, it's different with a baby on board. In other words, yes, Virginia, you do need some sort of plan for child care. Even if you're just working a few hours a day, or even just one day a week. You'll still need some guaranteed stretches of time to work, and most babies just do not approve of that idea.

Nope. They don't. At their regular baby conventions, they've voted on the matter, and decided they'd rather have you all to themselves, 24/7. This is a pact that babies have made with each other for eternity. Even those really cute Buddha babies. Put the receiver to your ear, start talking, and they start crying. (This is one of those behaviors that persists for the next sixteen years or so. Until they take over the phone.)

So face the facts and get some help.

It's terrific, of course, if you can coordinate with your spouse from the get-go, figuring out a schedule that works for all of you. I've had a few friends whose husbands saved up their vacation or personal time until fairly late into their leave, and then the guys stayed home with the baby—or baby and Mom—so Mom could get some work done. It can be a wonderful experience all around. "My husband was with a big company and had plenty of personal and vacation time saved up, so he took four weeks to stay home with our son. It was great for him. He had total responsibility for him all day while I worked," says Lisa. "I think he had more fun than I did during the leave. He strapped Tim in the baby carrier and took walks in the park. They had a great time."

If you don't have a hubby with time to spare or a mom, sister, or mother-in-law in the wings, don't despair. Working at home may still work out. Many of my friends were delighted that they started using child care before they went back to work, because they could do it gradually and be right there, in case it didn't work out. And nearly every one of them was grateful for the chance to get to know her child's caregiver before she had to start work again and also for the chance to start the separation from her baby gradually. "I couldn't imagine how I was going to leave Sarah, and it was so hard the first morning when I did. But since I knew I had to do it, this seemed to be the best way. I was nearby, just down the block, I could check up on things, and she didn't have to go the whole day without me," says Mary, an attorney in the Midwest. "And even better, I didn't have to go the whole day without seeing her!"

Women I know who decided to work during their leaves have chosen various ways to handle child care at this stage. Some of them took their babies to a neighbor who watched kids in the neighborhood for a living. Others found a part-time caregiver to come to the house. A few shared a caregiver with friends, turning what might have been a marginal, part-time job for the right caregiver into a better, higher-paying full-time one. Virtually no one used a child-care center. Most child-care centers won't take very young babies, and with good reason. Tiny infants do not yet have much immunity to many common diseases, so it's best to keep your baby home for as long as you can.

One note of caution, however. If you plan to have someone care for your baby while you're trying to get work done, don't forget all those stories I keep telling you about colicky and unpredictable babies and the general chaos that follows in the wake of a newborn. I experienced all of those things with both my kids. Also separation anxiety, as they got a little older. Dan was relatively easy on this front: he didn't feel the need to bawl his eyes out every time I walked away from him.

But Rachel started to show separation anxiety when she was just four months old, at a time when I was trying to write in my home office. Cacilda, a wonderful Brazilian grandmother from the neighborhood, came in to help me out a couple hours a day. But we soon learned that Rachel would shriek every time she saw me and I didn't pick her up. And that was a trauma for all of us—Rachel, Cacilda, and me.

I solved this dilemma by learning to skulk around the apartment, flush to the walls, darting across doorways, always checking to see if the coast was clear, so Rachel wouldn't see me when they were playing inside. We all survived. And I still feel lucky to have had the chance to keep her at home and ease back to work gradually. But there were certainly days when I knew I should have my head examined. No one in her right mind would try to work this way, I'd tell myself. I'd answer myself by saying, well, skulking is not exactly quality time, but it was better, in the long run, than rushing back to work!

As Time Goes By

Sooner or later, you're going to be thinking a lot more about the end of your maternity leave and the transition ahead. By the fourth month, you might even miss work and adult conversation. You might even feel chatty, like you want to call the office, find out what's going on. You might even start planning to drop by. Even show off that baby of yours.

But don't expect to be your old self.

You're not your old self.

You're a new parent.

And if you don't watch it, you're going to change all the perceptions of you at work in a new way. You may be seen as a bore. A relatively nice one, but still, a time-consuming bore.

It will start because everyone will ask you about the baby. It's only polite.

And then you answer. And then, you start gushing. Even to your boss. You can't help it, because you haven't stopped to think about how it all sounds to everyone else. So you give the complete report. About how your baby just held his head up *all by himself!* Or reached, grabbed, and held a rattle for a *whole minute!* Or about the way your husband got that baby to *laugh out loud!*

Depending on your boss and your company, a little of this may be perfectly acceptable. For a few minutes, anyway. Everyone understands that babies are darn amazing. Especially your own. Or at least everyone understands that babies are *supposed* to be darn amazing. At least to their parents. So it's only polite to inquire. How is that baby? they ask.

But remember, inside and outside the workplace, no one is quite as impressed by your baby as you are. Try to take the cue when your boss's eyes start to wander, or she changes the subject or starts to rifle through some papers on her desk. That means it's time to get back to the topic of work, how much you're looking forward to your return (even if you're not) and how great the company is for giving you all this time off.

And if you've actually got your baby in tow, as the anxious and proud new mom, be sensitive to everyone's workload, interest, and ability to enjoy your progeny. Remember that even if they adore you and your baby, they are at work and may have deadlines pressing at them. They can't linger the way they would on a truly social visit. Be especially brief with your boss, no matter how polite and excited he seems. More than anyone, he's likely to have work pulling at him. And if the baby starts to fuss or needs to nurse, even if it's only two seconds after you sat down, just excuse yourself with a smile. It's far better to err on the side of being too respectful than to turn into the office boor, with everyone afraid to ask you even one question about that baby, for fear of hearing one of your monologues.

No doubt you do have some friends at work who will adore hearing all the details, are eager to know how you are getting along, and want to linger over the baby and make just the right kind of fuss. Those are the ones to call in advance and arrange a lunch date or coffee break outside the office, so you can gush with abandon. These are your real friends, the ones you'll see even after you quit this job.

For the rest, be as reciprocal as you can be. Many will be truly delighted to see you happy, even radiant, about your new life. They will also be delighted when you can take at least a passing interest in them and their concerns. So when you're visiting, be prepared for the moments when your supervisor starts to fill you in, with great gusto, about her latest project, how well the department is doing, and all the kudos they're earning from the higher-ups. Remember, you used to be interested in this stuff. This is your job, and they know you as a coworker.

So even though you can barely track the conversation once you see where it's going, discipline yourself. Remember that you are still suffering new-mommy-itis, a state that often makes it hard to listen to anything except baby stories. It's a temporary state and you don't want to insult your boss. In fact, you'll likely regain your interest in work again someday soon. Maybe even by the time you get back to your job.

Nod your head, congratulate her.

Tell her you can't wait to get back.

Then go home, and enjoy that baby.

After all, you may not have too much time left. And now you can walk, talk, and sit in a chair without pain.

Chapter 8

Finding Time for Yourself

When Rachel was just eight weeks old, I put her in a Snugli, folded my Aprica stroller, and boarded a crosstown bus in Manhattan, bound for a postpartum exercise class at a local Y. Total time on the bus, maybe twelve minutes. Not a huge adventure, unless you're a first-time mother. That was me.

It was my first bus excursion with Rachel, and I was terrified she would awaken and shriek, and drive everyone around me crazy. Also, there were the fumes from the bus. I didn't want her inhaling them. And I'd never ridden to this particular stop. I asked the bus driver to call it out for me, so I wouldn't miss it. I made the request even knowing it's something most New York bus drivers frown upon. It means they have to take an active interest in bus riders. Nor is it a practice that New York bus riders generally applaud. As noisy as the city might be, commuters put a premium on their privacy, reading the paper uninterrupted, staring into space uninterrupted, or even talking loudly to their own friends, uninterrupted. Only out-of-towners have to have their stops yelled out, interrupting all these critical activities.

As a New Yorker myself at the time, I knew all this. But as a new mother, I felt I'd entered combat. Riding across town on a city bus was a major new undertaking, and I needed someone to make sure I got off when I needed to, even if Rachel was shrieking. Especially if Rachel was shrieking.

Rachel slept the entire, very long twelve minutes.

And I got off at the wrong stop.

Having successfully tensed every muscle in my body, I spent the twelve minutes on red alert, ready to leap up, grab the stroller, and make an ungraceful exit at the first bark from the bus driver. In my state of heightened tension, I missed a critical detail. When the bus driver barked, it was for the elderly lady I nearly knocked over with the stroller, who needed a stop ahead of mine.

I did not figure this out until I was on the sidewalk, still two blocks from my destination. Sweating and puffing with my extra twenty pounds of weight, I loaded Rachel into the stroller, slung the diaper bag and purse over my shoulder, and lumbered on to the Y, almost late for my first dose of "self time."

Taking an exercise class a few months after childbirth was exactly the sort of thing that every women's magazine, every new mother's book, every friend, and most especially every other experienced mother I knew (maybe two at that time) recommended.

Of course, I had my doubts, since I had my doubts about everything at the time, and was usually ready to reconsider most any decision that I'd made, immediately upon making it. Luckily, I was late enough this time that I didn't have time to change my mind. I passed Rachel off to the young women in the "child care" room right off the gym where my class was to be held. The young women in charge seemed used to mothers like me, and immediately acquiesced to my insistent demand that they come and get me *immediately* if Rachel started to cry. (She slept through the whole class.)

Once in the class, lying on a mat on the floor, I remembered a critical fact. I am not an exercise person. At least not an indoor-organized-class exercise person. Walks outside, hiking, even jogging outside was okay. Reading, going to movies, meeting friends for coffee or a glass of wine, even better. This, of course, was indoor-organized-class exercising. And it immediately called up all the other experiences I'd had of being in a gym that smelled like a gym, with an instructor yelling out instructions that I had no hope of following. Inevitably, the experience calls up my happily repressed memories of prepuberty gym classes, the days when I had to wear Chubbette clothes because I'd gotten chubby in the middle, couldn't climb ropes, or do pull-ups, or do as many sit-ups as American presidents seemed to think I should be able to do. Or so my gym teachers told me.

Just before the instructor began, I was thinking that this particular indoor-organized-exercise experience was the closest approximation of the prepuberty days I'd had in a while. Here I was with my flabby abdomen, flabby hips, and no real athletic ability that I knew of, about to endure yet another instructor trying to walk me through moves that I probably couldn't do. This experience had the added allure of my seeing that two thirds of my classmates were groomed in the ways of Manhattan. Slim, even wearing makeup, I thought. It wasn't clear to me that they could be postpartum. I weakly smiled at the only other mom, a few feet away, who also had a postpartum stomach rising beneath her baggy sweats. We'd both chosen the baggy sweats, where the other women sported leotards. Tights. I couldn't imagine that.

Then the instructor began.

"Close your eyes," she said.

Okay, I thought. I can do that.

"Now make every part of your body as heavy as you can. Sink into the mat. Your arms, your legs, your back, your head. Relax every part of your body."

Okay, I thought. I can do that too.

"Now I want you to tense every muscle in your body, and then relax. Start with your fists. Hold them tight to the count of ten. Now release."

I could do that too. And so it went, until I had tensed and then released my entire body twice. Then it was back to sinking into the mat. And staying as quiet as I could, just as she directed. Then clearing my mind. Focusing on the moment.

"Many new moms don't recognize the tension they carry around with them," the instructor said. "That's why I start this way, to show you how to let it go."

Not recognize? This little exercise made me realize I was mind-numbingly ignorant of the level of tension I'd been holding in. It must have been the first time in eight weeks I'd been so relaxed. My body was grateful, and so was my mind.

She then asked us to breathe deeply, and focus on being somewhere that we found relaxing. Very much like what I'd learned in Lamaze class. I remembered how much I liked the breathing, and the focus. I took a breath, exhaled slowly, and put myself on the top of a peak in the Cascade Mountains, outside Seattle, where I'd backpacked as a teenager. Watching the sunrise. In the kind of silence you find only in deep wilderness. My body relaxed even more.

The instructor then followed with twenty minutes of the stretching and muscle exercises that I'd expected. I could do maybe three of the twenty. But she did not push us. Instead, she let us go at our own pace, and warned us to listen to our bodies, to be gentle with ourselves, to know that it would take some time to recover from childbirth and regain our former mobility. It will come, she assured us.

She was kind to us, and her voice reminded me to be kind to myself. Don't rush it. Above all, don't injure yourself if you've had a cesarean, which I had. It felt good to be careful with myself. I was grateful to her for this simple lesson. That I should be kind to myself.

The class ended again with a wonderful relaxation exercise. After it was over, I lay on my mat an extra minute while everyone else got up to leave. "The class is over," the instructor informed me.

I was not even embarrassed. It didn't matter that she had to shoo me out, that I was even foolish now. It wouldn't matter if the bus driver barked, if Rachel shrieked on the ride home, if I ran the stroller over someone's toes or missed my stop. I was blissfully relaxed.

So, I thought to myself, this is what people mean. This is why people say it's important to take time for yourself. I was refreshed. I might even be able to laugh at a joke!

And it was probably the first time I'd felt that way in eight weeks. Not that I'd been so miserable. I'd had plenty of highs. Moments of real joy. But I hadn't been relaxed. I hadn't even realized how tense I was. Just as the instructor said. I'd just carried it around in my body. Being tense had become second nature to me.

If I'd kept my body and muscles on that kind of alert for too much longer, making even a simple bus ride into the equivalent of a suicide mission against Saddam Hussein, I'd probably collapse before Rachel reached toddlerhood. I wouldn't even be able to care for her.

Ironically, I'd be doing this in pursuit of being a Good Mother.

Cult of Sacrifice

I'm imagining that you've even heard the advice about taking time for yourself before. That you might have skimmed through the books on maternity leave or on the first year after the birth that always tell you to sleep when the baby sleeps and find time for yourself. In other words, I'm willing to admit that you might already have heard of this idea before you started reading this fabulous book. You might have even tucked the advice away somewhere in your consciousness, thinking it was worth remembering. Advice you could use.

Once you have the time.

But not right now, you tell yourself, if you tell yourself anything at all. For the first few weeks of maternity leave, the idea of finding any time for yourself may simply sound preposterous. You've hit the ground running, without time for reflection. At times, you feel almost robotic, responding to your baby's command-and-control system, which feels as though it must be hard-wired to your body. You even witness it operating. She cries and your milk lets down. She cries, and then quiets when she hears your voice.

You're grateful for the full fifteen minutes here and there when no one needs you. If you get a whole hour, you're delirious. But you haven't made a real plan to capture time for yourself. It seems impossible, and most of the time you try not to mind it. Even when it's crazy and you're crazy-tired, you just tell yourself that now you are a mother and mothers don't always have time for themselves. This baby needs you and that's that. You may have an idea that it will ease up. A vague notion that you'll get around to those activities you like to do on maternity leave. That you'll take a break.

When there's time.

Of course, you might get lucky, as I did, and wind up at an exercise class run by a really good postpartum exercise instructor like mine. And then you might get smart enough to try to find that time sooner than later.

And once you do, you'll understand why all those editors and experts harp on the idea that it's so important to create high-quality time for yourself once you become a mother. Repeating it, and repeating it, and repeating it is the only way to counter that big surround-sound message that most of us get the moment that we hold our first baby doll, the message that motherhood is all about sacrifice, that the good mother gives up everything for her kids. Even herself.

It's a hard message to counter because tiny babies are so dependent, and they really do need you. So giving up all your normal activities, all your time and all your attention, does seem like a perfectly reasonable approach to motherhood. In fact, during the first few weeks, it's a survival strategy for you and your baby. But keep your mind attuned to the idea that it's good to move out of this mode as soon as you and your baby are ready.

And it may also be helpful to know that the lesson doesn't always come neatly packaged. But it will come. I'm just suggesting that you do it the lower-stress way. That you get yourself to an exercise class, go out for coffee with a friend, or just take a walk, so that you don't have to take the alternate route to this insight.

The alternative route is not really one you want to take, as so many of my friends report. The epiphany arrives via a mini–nervous breakdown, at an exasperated moment when new mothers began to think they really *do* understand child abuse and runaway mothers. I tell you this in case you don't bump into someone like my enlightened exercise instructor. It's so you'll know that what you're experiencing is not a nervous breakdown but the simple return of sanity, of natural separation, of your mind and body letting you know that it's time to get back into the world again, time to organize your post-baby life in a new way, a way that will meet everyone's needs, including your own.

It starts with learning to take twenty-minute breaks, getting out of the house for a quick walk, or just learning to lie down when the baby's sleeping instead of doing things around the house. (I didn't figure that out, and neither did a lot of my friends, until the second child. But I'm trying to convince you not to wait that long.)

But after you learn to do that, you'll find that creating time for your new self to unfold—what I call "new-self-time"—a process that starts while you are on maternity leave, is not quite so simple as it sounds. It's not just a matter of taking time, getting those twenty-minute breaks. It's making time for your new self; it's figuring out who that new self is, now that you're a mom. In fact, part of what's wearing you out is trying to figure out who your new self is.

It starts with all those wild emotions, which signal the huge change in your life, the big transition under way. It doesn't happen all at once, but you do feel a new self emerging, with new values and priorities.

And that new self may require a whole new set of activities, new sources of satisfaction, new ways to relax, and new ways to be. Now that you are a mom. Now that you have a job *and* a baby. What you are beginning to understand is that you are going to have to invent a new schedule, not just add on to the old one. You are going to have to find enough time for work, your marriage, your baby, and the other things that are important to you.

Including yourself.

And that usually takes some effort, some time to get the vision, to piece things together, to invent this new life as a working mom.

For my friend Cynthia, the moment of truth came several months after the birth of her son, when she collapsed in a heap on the bed, ready to scream at anyone or anything that moved. Especially her baby, her husband, and the dog. Not that she would have actually screamed at them. It was just how she felt as she lay on the bed. Maybe she just wanted to scream, at no one in particular.

To any relatively calm and objective observer, it wouldn't have taken long to get to the root of Cynthia's mood. But for her, a competent woman who thrived on being in charge, it took some tears and some talking. In fact, it took her by surprise to find herself suddenly weeping on the bed. And then "it took lots of talking" to her very understanding mate, "to understand what was bothering me." The ultimate diagnosis was simple. "I had lost all personal time."

"I was taking care of the baby, cooking, cleaning, or collapsing in exhaustion," she says. "I was trying to do too much during the day at home."

To move forward, to feel better, she and her husband had to do more than talk. They had to work out a new schedule, one that got her more help with the chores and got both of them more time to do the things they loved.

Listening to Cynthia and my other friends, I see there is a certain sanity in those moments of insanity, the ones where you collapse or scream or yell. Or find yourself, as I did, such a ridiculous ball of nerves that you can't even ride a bus without making it into a Big Deal. These moments of seeing the problem come only when you are finally ready for them. Usually, that's when your baby is sleeping more, going longer between feedings and changings.

For me, it came at a predictable time. I was ready for an exercise class at eight weeks, the moment almost to the clock that doctors say that my body should be nearly recovered from a cesarian delivery. But there's no telling exactly when your moment will come. Part of it depends on your baby. It really is hard to make time for yourself until that baby is settled. For some women, it's hard to do much of anything until the baby's sleeping through the night. So I tell you to be ready to make time for yourself, to explore your new self, to begin to create your new life, but also be gentle with yourself. Don't make things worse by trying to follow someone else's rules or duplicate someone else's experience.

Margery always keeps me in mind of this when she recalls how everyone told her to relax and get her baby out of her hair within two months. But her baby didn't sleep. "Yours will sleep through the night when she's ready, not when you, your mother or mother-in-law, or your pediatrician thinks he should. Babies do it when they're ready," says my friend Val, "and almost always when you're *more* than ready."

But whenever that happens, it's time to take inventory of how you're spending your time, how well you're taking care of yourself, what you want to add and what you want to leave behind now that you're a parent.

Whether you do it at exercise class, as I did, or in a heap on the bed, as Cynthia did, it's a key part of your journey, a time to align the new you with your new life, to let go of the pre-baby you and figure out how you want to spend your time and what kind of time you'll have from here on out as a working mom.

Above all, to realize that you are a new self. So when you start thinking about creating time for yourself, you're going to have to explore who that self is. It may feel like a puzzle at first, matching time, activities, joy, companionship, all those sources of renewal, to that new self. To the working-mother self.

With a job, a baby, a significant other, a mortgage, a car, the in-laws, your parents, and your friends, this is an exercise you can't afford to skip. You don't have to do it on an exercise mat. You don't have to do it weeping on the bed, in great turmoil.

But you do have to do it, so you can savor the moments ahead.

It starts with those little bits and pieces that you create in the beginning. The walk, the nap, the conversation with a friend. The women's magazine editors have that right. You do need the breaks from the relentless demands of an infant, to breathe, to get perspective, to rest. "I found that when I took a break from Ben, even if it was just fifteen or twenty minutes, I came back to him more excited, more appreciative, just glad to be with him," says Teri. "After maternity leave, I turned that twenty minutes into one night a week, out on my own, to do whatever I liked. And Michael does the same thing," she adds. "It keeps us both sane, and happy to see each other."

My friends also say that they've discovered what I discovered, that one of the important things about the "self-time" after a baby is that it isn't always alone time, not strictly time only for you. It might be, but it doesn't have to be. Gradually, you come to see that there has to be some time for the new self, time to discover the new ways you want to spend time, the new things that bring you joy. It is time for you, but not always time alone. And it is time for the new you, the one who is now a mom.

It might be better-time-with-baby. Or it might be time-with-friends or time-for-a-movie or time-for-your-favorite-pastry at a local bakery. Or pizza-with-your-hubby. Or that ever-recommended-bubble-bath so highly touted in the women's magazines.

For me, "new-self-time" was a walk. Just stepping out-doors, getting out of the apartment. Walking past the shop windows in my Manhattan neighborhood. Or walking in Riverside Park. But it was also adult conversation, a long-distance talk with an old friend, someone I'd known since high school, and someone who was a mother and also knew me in all my incarnations. Someone who understood and appreciated me as I laid claim to my new self.

Getting time for yourself also means getting rid of the stuff that eats up your time and makes you feel bad. It's jettisoning time spent doing things you really don't want to do. It's learning not to sacrifice too much. Not picking up your husband's shirts, or not doing the laundry, or not doing the grocery shopping. Not for a few months. It's assigning those tasks to your hubby or someone else. Even paying for some of it, if you can.

In other words, you have to relearn what will feed your soul, rather than diminish it, now that you are a mom and a soon-to-be-back-at-work mom. When I look back, I can see that what I did, and everyone else I knew did, was to try to find the things that would enlarge my days, remind me of why I wanted to be a parent. I needed things that provided a slight escape from the routines, from the demands that kept me in ragged motion.

It was finding a balance, finding a new way to be my new self.

To do that, I had to make some choices. And I had to get some help.

Taking Inventory

Finding time for yourself doesn't follow a formula; it's not just the time off from routines that you take, although that matters. You do need breaks. You do need to relax.

But more, you need to take an inventory of sorts, hope-fully sometime before you go back to work, of how your life is working now and how it will work into the future. You need to identify what's working and what's not working for this new self, this new mother self: what's feeding it and what's draining it.

That means understanding just what creates the tension when you get on a crosstown bus or collapse on the bed. It could be that you have been truly ignoring your needs, say, sewing curtains as I did for Rachel's room, and failing to take a nap when you really *really* need one. Those of us who've been through it know how hard it is to do. That's why we're always telling our friends to listen to this one piece of advice, to take time for yourself, to make time for yourself, and above all not to throw away time for yourself. My friend Susan recently confessed she'd spent the wee hours of the night paying bills one night on her maternity leave, while the baby slept. "That was stupid! *Stupid!*" she says. "I see that now. I needed to sleep. But I was so focused on getting something done. I just let my own needs go."

But it may not just be stupidity. It could be that you aren't getting the help you need. That you are not tending to yourself because you have yet to reorganize your commitments to match the new you. Someone else, like your mate, could pay the bills. Your sister or sister-in-law or mother or very good friend can run to the store so you can get a nap. Takeout food tastes good and can take the heat off for dinner. In fact, your hubby can pick it up on the way home.

This sounds pretty simple. You may even expect to eat takeout and ask for help before you start maternity leave. But very often, a whole new way of thinking emerges on leave. You're the one home, so you feel and everyone else feels that you're the one in charge of the home front. Since you and your husband have never been through this before, you may both even assume you're the one with time to do it all: The housework, the errands, the shopping, and the night feedings.

Sure, you might get some help the first week. Even a lot of attention. But then, after a few weeks, the baby settles and everyone disappears. Your hubby, your mom, the in-laws, friends. You're the one staring at the dirty dishes, the laundry, the tumbleweeds growing under the couch. So you just start taking care of it.

And soon, this habit of doing it all and not getting help, not sharing the child care and the chores, turns into the cause of your tension. It's objective fact that you really *don't* have the time for yourself, not even twenty minutes. And it will stay that way until you begin to take inventory, reorganize your commitments, and get help if you need it.

Doing it all is a common and a deadly pattern that you want to avoid establishing, and if it is starting to get established, you definitely want to break it, before you get back to work.

Let me repeat that.

Your doing it all—the chores, the child care, the errands, the night feedings—is a common and a deadly pattern that you want to change. It can feel good for a while, even competent. Your husband may praise you endlessly for what a good job you're doing, how great the baby is, how wonderful it is that you're home.

But you won't be there much longer. Soon you're going to be back at work, and if you stay on this track, it's only going to get worse. The lack of time.

It's what Cynthia recognized, as she began to sort out her feelings after that fit of lying on the bed and wanting to scream at everyone. She and her husband sat down and made a list of everything that *had* to be done around the house, and everything they *wanted* to do every week. Within a few days, they came up with a new weekly schedule, one that gave each of them responsibility for certain chores as well as one night off a week, to do whatever they wanted to do.

This list making is a good exercise, especially because it begins to reveal the mechanics of your new life, the one you are going to live as a working mother. Some of the old rituals—lazing around on Sunday mornings, brunch at a local restaurant, dinners out with single friends, Saturday nights at the movies—may be lost. Or they may fade slowly, as they did for me. At first, and especially with only one child, you may find that you can still cart that baby around and carry on some things the way you did when you were childless.

But over time, the changes will assert themselves. Most certainly, you will have less time for everything you did before —and more new things to do. You can't just paste the new things on, like time to take care of the baby. You have to get rid of some old things, make choices. Since you inevitably have more to do, it's the only way to fit everything in.

What's the first to go? Most likely you've heard by now that you have to stop being a perfectionist, just let the house go, relax your standards.

That's probably the worst advice on the planet. Once you have kids, you're going to see a gradual and ultimately dramatic increase in both the volume of housework and the necessity for getting it done. At the beginning it's only a pacifier or soft, stuffed animal on the floor that you trip over. But tomorrow, it will be plastic action figures that really hurt your feet. Play-Doh that crumbles and squishes into the floor and the carpets. Food on the floor. Dirty diapers and dirty clothes.

So you can't let the house go. Once I had Rachel, I saw that if we didn't keep up with things, we'd never be able to get across a room without tripping on toys or baby equipment, we'd all have to go naked for want of clean clothes, and the house would smell worse than skunks.

The real secret for finding and keeping time for yourself, starting right on maternity leave, is to get organized, set new priorities, and get help. This, of course, is not as easy as it sounds. First of all, a lot of this stuff is considered "women's work." Next, we are the ones at home. And last, nobody really wants to get too intimate with the toilet bowl. Not most of us. So it takes a lot of effort to change things—more than anything, it requires your attention. In the beginning, as you go through this transition, you're going to have to spend time just thinking about how you spend your time. Now and into the future.

My friend Bonnie, a social worker, runs support groups for moms, and one of her favorite exercises is to get them to just sit down and write down everything they do and how much time it takes. She makes them include all aspects of every task, especially the time it takes to plan and think a task through. "When they tell me that dinner takes one hour, I remind them that most of them probably also spend time thinking of whether the food they're serving is nutritious, finding recipes to keep things interesting, preparing at least a mental grocery list, and then actually doing the shopping before they even start to cook," she says. "Too often they underestimate the time things take."

Same with child care. "All they think about is the time it took to interview someone or go look at a few places. They forget about all the time they spent researching what good care looks like, finding out where the good places and good people are from friends and coworkers, and then making a lot of calls, before they ever get to the point of actually interviewing anyone," she says.

Once moms get a real-time view of their lives, she says, they "fully appreciate everything they do—and. more important, they get help."

What You Want to Do

And then there's the little matter of figuring out what you want to do. For you as a new mother, self-time may turn out to be spending time with other mothers, swapping war stories, getting reassurance, especially finding out that, no, you're not the only one who didn't know how to pick out the right diaper and put it on properly. And, yes, real mothers do get fed up. That kind of time can instantly make you feel less fed up. In fact, all my friends have found, through a formal support group or through their own informal network, that one of the most important times for themselves was the time spent with friends, digesting and talking about their new selves.

I still can recall, and with great appreciation, the parent meetings I went to at Basic Trust Infant and Toddler Center, a child-care center in Manhattan, during Rachel's first year. These meetings focused on the stuff we really cared about. Instead of talking about the center's business or fund-raising or hearing lectures on How to Be a Good Parent, we heard from each other. The topics were always Feeding, Sleeping, and Children's Weird and Outrageous Behavior.

Peggy Sradnick, the director, would start off the meetings by asking, "Anyone having any issues around eating?" and the floodgates would open, everyone with their own story about kids who didn't eat, or ate too much, or only ate a few things or wanted to eat everything. Projectile vomiting.

Then on we'd go to sleeping and crying. There was the night when one of the moms confessed that she'd yelled at her kids. She said it with such feeling, a tinge of humiliation, that I kept quiet and waited to see what everyone else would say. I'm not a yeller, but I'd certainly wanted to yell. The entire room was momentarily silent, until Sarah, one of the moms, just jumped in, "Yell? Yell? I've yelled so much I've lost my credibility. It's totally ineffective. I'm looking for a new strategy."

The whole room laughed, relieved. Then she added another nugget. "Oh, and my older kids are now four. They're twins. And I don't care what the experts say. I've come to one conclusion as a parent. Do whatever works. Whatever works. That's what I'm looking for. Something that works."

Now the relief that flowed through the room was palpable. It reminds me today of the Baby Blues cartoon book entitled *I Should Only Have to Scream Once.* Looking back, I realize how glad I was, how glad we all were, to have a place where we could be ourselves, explore who these new selves were, how we wanted to parent.

Which brings me to the other piece of advice that you're going to hear a lot as a new parent. When people tell you to find some time for yourself, they also mean some time to learn about this new self. When they say isolation is a problem, that you need to get out, that you need to find friends and support, what they mean is that you need to find fellow travelers, people on the same path at the same time, with the same values you have.

You might find those folks in your postpartum exercise class, as a lot of my friends did. Or you might sign up for a "Mommy and me" class—organized play groups for new moms, at the local Y or a new mother's support group at your church or even at a local women's center. Some hospitals and pediatricians post notices or have information about such support groups. You might even find some leads on the Web. Many of the Web sites designed for women include links to national groups that, like La Leche League, have local chapters.

But don't stay on the Web. Get out and talk to people in person. There's nothing like the give-and-take, the conversation, and the camaraderie of friendship to feed the self. These conversations can be deeply validating, times that truly feed your soul.

If you're as energetic as some of my friends, you might even start a group yourself. My friend Leslie organized a walking group of new moms. They met at a particular place in their town, at the same time, every day. Whoever showed up, walked. The group of four women changed a little from day to day, but there were always at least two. When the weather got bad, they went for coffee or walked in a local mall. Another friend organized a group of new moms to exercise together at their homes. They bought an exercise video, took that and their babies from house to house, did their exercising for free, and got to talk with each other on the side.

I'm not one for organized classes, but I loved meeting my friends for coffee at a Greek coffee shop near my apartment. Or in the park, just to push the babies in the strollers or sun our faces while we sat on a bench.

All of that was definitely self-time, time that helped me grow into my new self, discover what it meant to be a parent and how I wanted to be a parent.

Getting Your Body Back

Of course, there's also the physical self, the one that's changed so radically since you got pregnant and gave birth that you may not feel like it's you anymore. If you are nursing, you may not even feel as though your body is really yours. For a while, it's something you share with your baby.

But over time you inevitably come to terms with your new shape. I recently heard from a friend who describes a moment when her child was fifteen months old, that she looked at herself in the mirror and decided it was time to lose the twenty-one pounds she still had hanging on her hips. She signed up for an exercise class, threw out all the junk food in her house, and began to snack on carrots and celery. Within two months, "I was back to my pre-baby, size six self." And that, she says, boosted her spirits and her confidence.

I am certain that it would, even though I have not been a size 6 since I was six years old. But I do remember that by the end of my maternity leave, I wanted my body back. I didn't live on carrots, but I did begin to walk more, and gradually even took up jogging again. By the time I was ready for a second child, I'd lost all the weight and I had taken up a regular exercise routine.

I say all this because what I see among my friends is that weight and body changes are just as personal as everything else that goes into the kind of mother you'll be. And as a working woman, you may find yourself thinking about it even more and even sooner than your stay-at-home friends. You have to get back into professional clothes, be in a work environment again. That drove some of my friends to be more concerned about shrinking their bodies back down. Getting a flat stomach was also part of the self they wanted to keep as a new mom. Staying slim kept them confident.

They signed up for exercise classes, went for walks, rented exercise videos. They cut out the fat and the snack foods at home. It's not rocket science, but it does take discipline and most of them managed to lose most of the weight they gained by the time their babies reached six months.

It took me a year, but it wasn't top-of-mind for me. Once through my dreary puberty, I'd been average, size 10 dress, size 8 shoes, height five feet four. Always average, never a standout, and no one made an issue of my weight. I didn't like the extra weight I carried around much, but I felt confident I'd lose it over time.

My point is that some new moms—and you may be one of them—will devote a good deal of their self-time to a regular exercise routine. Most experts recommend this, of course, since it enhances your health and reduces stress. Nearly every mom I know who has made exercise part of her routine, from swimming to walks to weightlifting, is grateful that she did. Just as the experts advise.

So if you haven't tried it yet, you might want to consider it as part of your new routine as a mother. Like me, you may find that the stress just flows right out of you, that you relax after an exercise class, a walk in the park, even a walk down the block.

Accepting the New You

But the most important thing is to do the things that make you feel good, things that help you discover the new you and make your new life work the way you want it to.

To do that, you have to get rid of the things you don't have to do, don't like to do, and don't need to do. You have to find the things you want to do, the old ones and the new ones. You might go back to swimming two evenings a week while your husband cares for the baby. Or you might go out one night a week with your friends for a drink, just to compare notes and let off steam.

And then there are all the things you never imagined that you'd do, that you now want to make time for. Like watching your baby learn to roll over . . . sit up . . . walk.

Later it's going to Rug Rats movies or watching Cartoon Network. Me, I never imagined I'd like watching *Sponge Bob Square Pants,* a quirky new-age half-hour cartoon show on Cartoon Network so much. I didn't even know it existed before I had kids. And before my niece had her kids. And now it's one of my favorite things. That's how it is. You grow into a new self, and learn things you never imagined. You may like *Blue's Clues,* a more conventional, sweeter kids' show. Me, I go for *Sponge Bob.* It's one of those things I make time for. Things that feed the soul. Like laughing with my kids.

Chapter 9

Whom Can You Trust to Care For This Baby?

I awoke at 3 A.M., in a sweat. I'd had Daniel a mere three months before, and now, in just four weeks, I had to start working again. I had to find child care.

I hadn't expected this reaction. After all, he was my second child and I'd already been through a search for child care for a new baby. And this time, I knew I wouldn't face the predictable inquisition, from relatives and even friends, about using a child-care center for my infant: "Couldn't you get someone to come to the house?" people would ask. "Isn't it a l-o-o-n-n-g day for her?" Their pointed questions and tone conveyed in no uncertain terms that they knew, just knew, Rachel would contract bubonic plague at the center I chose for her. Or scabies.

At least this time, I wouldn't face those queries. Our family circumstances had changed dramatically. We now lived in Jersey City, for one thing, and there were no good child-care centers nearby. With a long commute to work, and a second child to worry about after school, I'd decided to hire a nanny. In fact, I had an interview with my first applicant in just six hours.

Six very short hours away.

I sat straight up in bed and looked over at Dan, asleep in his cradle. Suddenly, a nanny seemed like a foolish, foolish idea.

What if she kidnapped him?

What if she snatched Daniel first thing one sunny morning, right after I left for my job? By afternoon, she could be in Los Angeles. Or London. Venezuela. Tunisia.

How would I find her and my boy?

My God, what if she gave me a phony identity? Just so she could kidnap my boy. Then how would I find her? I'd read stories like that. Or at least I imagined I had. Maybe at the checkout stand at the local A&P. Or on a newsstand at the Port Authority Bus Terminal. Baby snatchers.

I began to sweat even more.

And I suddenly had to have Daniel right next to me. He was peaceful in his tiny wooden cradle, in a deep sleep I could only dream about. Still, I risked waking him by gently lifting him and taking him into bed with me. I kept him as close as I could, snuggling my face next to his head. His scalp was still smooth and soft, with only a few tufts of hair. I loved that feeling, even though we were both a little sweaty.

But my mind was still racing.

How could I have someone, someone I hadn't even met yet, come to the house to care for him? I'd have to install a major security system. With cameras in every room. Even the bathroom. You could get out the bathroom window if you tried.

I didn't even pause to consider the fact that the bathroom window downstairs was painted shut, and the one upstairs was, well, upstairs. Climbing out of it would mean a fifteen-foot drop. Who would do that, especially with the goal of trying to take a baby along?

At 3:30 A.M. those details didn't matter. In fact, they didn't even occur to me. All I knew was that I had had an epiphany. Probably it was God's will that I had awakened like this. I now knew, just knew, that I could never entrust Daniel to some stranger who came to the house every day. To someone who had keys to my house. What was I *thinking*? What a *preposterous* idea!

I resolved right then that when my interviewee arrived, I'd simply tell her I'd changed my mind. I'd tell her I was going to quit work and take care of Dan myself.

That was about as far as my bold new action plan carried me before I fell back to sleep with Dan nestled next to me.

At 9 A.M., Geeta Satnarine walked into my life, and every single worry faded, every muscle relaxed, every doubt was gone. There's no real way to explain Geeta without meeting her, except to say that she has an aura about her, a confidence and a joy that follows her everywhere. Even my kids have commented on it since.

And she loved Daniel. The first thing she wanted to do was hold him. She loved babies. She loved my baby. And that made me happy.

And of course, I could see she had no intention of kidnapping him.

Learning to Trust Yourself

My getting struck down by anxiety the second time should not have been so surprising. As a writer and editor with national magazines, I'd been reporting on this stuff for years, and I knew that all the experts say that parting with an infant, entrusting that tiny, helpless being into the care of someone else, is nothing short of traumatic for most new moms.

The anxiety attached to the process is just a sign of the deep love you feel for your new baby. In other words, these same experts remark that if you're *not* anxious, that is something you should probably get anxious about. It shouldn't be too easy to separate from your baby the first time, to entrust her to the care of others. It is considered part and parcel of mother love, a signal that you appreciate the harrowing new responsibility you have for this baby.

I don't think anyone has to tell us moms about that. It's enough to feel it in your gut. But it's good to be prepared for the full force of it, especially since finding child care usually isn't quite as simple as it was with Dan. It isn't usually just one night of intense jitters, and then you wake up, and, *poof,* there's the perfect person.

I'm going to tell you how it went with Rachel, just so you know I had to suffer a little more than that. It could make you feel better as you get into your own search. Also so you know that you don't always end up with the arrangement you expect.

It pays to keep an open mind, since a big part of your choice will be dictated by what's available out there. For example, you may wish for a Mary Poppins, someone who is loving but firm, who helps your child grow up healthy and happy, who teaches your child to *eat vegetables* and *clean up her room.* Or you may picture a grandmotherly figure: soft, patient, gentle, and full of knowledge from all the children she's already raised. Someone who can help you. Or maybe you fancy a younger woman, someone in her thirties, old enough to know something about the world and raising kids, but young enough to get down on the floor with your baby.

But then you go out and see what's out there. And you discover none of these fantasies have anything to do with the realities in your community. You will find someone, someone really great.

But not necessarily who you expected, or in the setting you expected. At least that's the way it's gone for me and most of my friends.

With Rachel I was totally freaked out, just as I was with Dan. Maybe more so, since she was my first. I didn't really like leaving her at all during the first three months after she was born. When I did, I rushed back sooner than I'd said to see if she was okay. (She always was.) When I took a shower, I'd often turn the water off in midstream to make sure she wasn't crying. (Mostly, she wasn't.)

So I was in an overly protective, not to mention pretty tired, state when I set out to find care for Rachel. At that time I didn't want or need full-time care. I was working from home, writing articles on a part-time basis. I was a little smug about that. I figured I'd get someone to come to the apartment to take care of her while I wrote. Everyone told me how ideal all this was, and of course, I agreed.

Right up until I put an ad for the position in the *Irish Echo,* the local paper in Manhattan that had become the child-care connection for many middle-class families. Caregivers placed ads. Families placed ads. I got more than twenty-five calls in response to mine, and interviewed at least eight or nine. Then, I sat down and cried.

It was clear to me, after the fact, that the "job" I was advertising was so low-paying, so part-time, so marginal, that I might have titled the ad "Desperately Seeking the Desperate." In another community, like the one where my brother lives in rural Rhode Island, I might have found someone to do the job. But in Manhattan the cost of living is ridiculously high and I was not even offering subsistence wages. The people who called were between jobs, couldn't get jobs, or seemed uncertain if they wanted a job at all. I considered taking a few straight to the local mental health center. There was one sweet young woman I considered just taking in altogether, because otherwise I feared she'd soon be homeless herself.

So I did not find a caregiver this way. But I did learn a valuable lesson, one worth sharing. I learned that I should have screened people on the phone. A simple enough idea if you have your wits about you. But I had no wits about me. I wasn't even quite sure what I would ask these people when they showed up for an interview. I thought meeting them might clarify things for me. So I had the people who could actually carry on a conversation show up for an interview, the eight or nine of them.

Now I know how smart it would have been to use that first phone call as a real interview, to narrow the field. You can do this whether you're hiring a nanny to come into your home or going to visit a center or someone at their home. Besides the usual questions, like what did they do before, and have they taken care of babies before, I learned it was good to ask very open-ended questions, questions that would just get them talking, and reveal who they are and why they want the job. Like why did they get into child care?

That's a good one, by the way. I had a couple of people who became so relaxed that they confessed they really didn't want to take care of kids. Child care was just something to tide them over until they got a "real" job. It was appalling to learn this when they were sitting in my apartment and Rachel was on my lap. Again, if I'd had my wits about me I might have asked them that simple question over the phone, before I had to hear this unsettling truth face to face.

I learned it's also an excellent question to ask of women who care for kids in their own homes. Many get into the child care business because they think it will be a good way to spend time with their own children and make a few bucks on the side, only to find that watching a group of kids drives them batty. And then they go out of business in a few months, leaving you in the lurch. The problem is so common in Oregon, in fact, that state officials recently began to require that all people who apply for a home child-care license take a course and learn what it's like before they get into it. The hope is to spare both these women the pain of doing a job they don't enjoy, and, for the parents like you and me, the dislocation and angst of losing a caregiver a few months after you sign on and get into your routines.

No matter what questions I asked or didn't, I did have enough wits to concede that my idea of a part-time caregiver coming to the apartment probably wasn't going to pan out. I needed another solution.

I then began to pursue leads from friends who told me about local women in the neighborhood who cared for babies and toddlers in their own apartments. Some weren't so pricey, and I thought maybe that could be a solution. Until I visited the only one who had an opening at that time. She was very sweet, and obviously cared about the two toddlers in her care, but the space was tiny and she had no toys or books. The apartment was on an air shaft, so it had no direct light. And a giant television sat in the living room. It wasn't on during my visit, but I suspected it would be the minute I left. I suspected it would be on all the time. There didn't seem to be much else to do.

Then I began to look into local child-care centers. Somehow, this seemed like a bad idea to me, the idea of dropping my little girl at a big, impersonal center. But I was now officially desperate and I had a couple friends who had used them, for babies as young as Rachel. One was wildly enthusiastic about the center she had sent her baby to, and I respected her. I liked her daughter, who was now two. So I decided to take a look for myself.

However, I didn't get to her center for my first look at a center because of scheduling problems. I went first to another that had a decent reputation, a few blocks away. Before this visit, I'd read a few brochures about how to evaluate group care and even jotted down a few things to look for. One of the main points was to be sure there were enough adults to care for the number of babies on hand.

But once I was inside this center, every rational thought vanished. The director was saying something to me, as she escorted me down a hallway to the infant room, but I couldn't pay attention—she could have been speaking Urdu or Greek for all I knew. All I could register was the noise level, and the size of the place. There were far more kids in this center than I'd expected, about a hundred in all, from ages six months to four.

She opened the door to the infant room, introduced me to the lead teacher, and left me to observe. It was quiet in here, which was a bit of a relief. Since there was no real furniture, I settled on the floor, which was covered with well-worn wall-to-wall carpeting. I thought that was probably a good sign, the fact that the room was conceived in a way that gave the babies and toddlers a lot of freedom. They could just crawl around.

But that was the only good feeling I had during my visit. I stayed for a half hour, and during that time, the teacher kept talking to me, not paying much mind to the babies crawling around on the floor. If one were insistent enough, she'd respond. But mostly she focused on me, and the babies focused on the colorful toys strewn on the floor. Or even got one of the books themselves, and managed to paw through it, gazing at the pictures. Or just gnawed on it.

As I took in this scene, every question my in-laws and my own mom had asked me about putting a baby into such a group situation flew into my mind. Maybe not every baby here had a runny nose and a cold that day (actually none of them did that I could see), but that's how it felt. It felt as though we were in a low-level fog of some kind—not the bubonic plague, but not healthy and nurturing, either. Just passing time.

Yet the odd part was that even after I left, I couldn't pinpoint exactly what was wrong. Like many new moms who have absolutely no faith in their own intelligence, I went down one of the checklists to see if I could identify what was missing. The ratios were good. The hygiene was okay. The toys were ones that babies could safely play with. I hadn't witnessed abuse, or even out-and-out neglect. And when I thought about how the teacher focused more on me than on the babies, I wondered if I were being too critical. She didn't *totally* ignore them. There were plenty of times at home when I talked on the phone while Rachel fussed a little. And this teacher had probably been instructed to talk to me, make sure my questions were answered.

Still, in my gut I knew that if this center were my only choice, I'd either quit working for a while or try to write articles while Rachel was napping. One of those desperate little plans new moms pull out of the air, as if they would work.

It is now quite clear to me as a more experienced mom what was wrong with that center. It was the pervasive alienation of the place, the lack of attention to the children. It was not outright neglect. I even knew people who had kids there who swore by the place. But my new-mom radar had picked up on how hungry the caregiver was to talk to me, rather than attend to the babies. It could have been poor pay, poor morale, and the problems that plague many centers. It could have been that this caregiver felt it was important to sell me on the place. Whatever, I knew that it didn't *feel* good, and wouldn't feel good to Rachel. I couldn't bear to think of her crawling aimlessly around, as the caregivers talked to visitors. When I got outside again, I was glad to be on the street, to breathe fresh air again, to have Rachel stashed in the Snugli.

And now I know, from both my friends and the expert research, how important such feelings are, for both you and your baby. In a good center, or any other setting, your baby's caregiver will be engaged with, responsive to, and caring about the children in her or his care, above all else. Nothing is more critical than that. Nothing. The experts call it "sensitivity" or "responsiveness" and they've come up with complicated ways to monitor and measure it. Some videotape caregivers, observe them and score the way they behave. Others send trained observers into child-care centers, to code the caregivers' responses.

What it all boils down to is that you want people who talk, sing, read, play, hold, comfort, cuddle, and roughhouse with your baby. People who are quick to respond when your baby cries. People who explain things to your child. People who show your baby new things. People who get excited when your baby does new things.

These are things that we all know in our gut, and now every early-childhood expert on the planet agrees. Studies conducted by the National Academy of Sciences, the National Institute of Child Health and Development, the National Institute of Mental Health, universities large and small, by professional groups representing early-childhood professionals and the American Academy of Pediatrics—all confirm what parents feel so deeply: that your baby must have enough love and attention if he is to learn and thrive.

When I didn't find that to be the case with the first child-care center I visited, I kept on looking. I didn't want to leave Rachel in the apartment with a mental patient (other than me). When I gave it some thought, I doubted I could work with her on my lap (definitely true). So I went to the next center on my list, Basic Trust Infant and Toddler Center, one I'd heard some very good things about. It was the one where my friend whom I respected enormously had put her baby at Rachel's age.

And just as with Geeta later, I knew from the moment I stepped over the threshold into the infant room that I'd arrived at the right place. The infant room was small and had a comfy couch at one end, big windows, a cooking and play area, and staff who obviously adored the kids. It didn't matter that this program was housed in a dingy public school, in a room that was quite worn. Once inside, you forgot about all that. This room felt like home.

Except the adults in charge knew a lot more about babies than I did at the time. Many of the teachers had a background in early-childhood development, I later found out. That's another sign of a good center. That people care enough about the children and their jobs to seek more knowledge and training.

I sank onto the couch with Rachel on my lap, talking to Wilma, a woman who'd already raised five kids of her own and still enjoyed being with babies. In fact, I had a hard time getting her attention when a baby crawled over to her, or one of the toddlers came over to say hello. Before long, she had two of them snuggled next to her, looking at a picture book. I loved the fact that she ignored me. I loved the affection she showed for the children. And at three months, Rachel obviously did as well. She kept pulling away from me, trying to get down on the floor and join the other babies.

Basic Trust was also living proof that a good child-care setting doesn't have to be elaborate or expensive. Babies are learning at a rapid pace, and their brains are developing in response to what they see, hear, touch, and feel. So it's important for them to have an interesting place to be every day. For babies, having some oatmeal to squish may translate into Living Large. Likewise books with pictures . . . toys that make noises . . . blocks to stack . . . a walk down the block. This center made a point of engaging kids in the kinds of activities they'd do in almost any household. Cook, play with toys, walk to the grocery store, the bank, the park.

I was sold on the place, but Basic Trust couldn't take Rachel until she was six months old. They just wouldn't have a spot open until then. That meant we had to find another solution for three months.

As luck would have it, that same week, beloved Cacilda, a Brazilian woman who had cared for other children in the neighborhood, came our way. It was one of those great serendipities that I have come to trust as a working mother. If you keep your circle big enough, trade favors, and help other people out, people help you. Not always the day you want them to, and not always the way you pictured, but things work out.

In this case, another family in the neighborhood had heard we were desperate for a part-time caregiver. They'd had Cacilda working for them for several years, but their youngest was off to school and they no longer needed her. And Cacilda didn't want a full-time job anymore. Then in her sixties, she'd had plenty of full-time jobs and could easily have gotten another. She obviously loved the work. So I called Cacilda. Just as Geeta would later take to Dan, Cacilda immediately took to Rachel. We arranged that she would come in part-time to take care of Rachel until we started her at Basic Trust. Within the first few days after she started working for us, I heard her singing to Rachel in Portuguese. My heart melted.

She was loyal and responsible beyond all reason. One fall day, a huge storm blew through Manhattan, knocking out power in many places and disrupting the bus line she usually took. I couldn't call her, since the phone was out. I certainly didn't expect her to show up. But suddenly she appeared at the door, without warning. She had walked across Central Park. "I knew you needed me today," was all she said. She knew I had a deadline for a story.

And so it went. Cacilda started the job with the understanding that her work with us would end in a few months, when Rachel started at Basic Trust. But things went so well with her and I couldn't bear to have Rachel out of the house so quickly, that we didn't start Basic Trust until Rachel was nine months old. And then I used Basic Trust only two days a week, and Cacilda for two other days, until Rachel was two.

Let Go of Your Fantasies

These details should help bring home to you how surprising the search for child care can be, how you might find something in a place you never expected to, that the great situation you do find may not match a single fantasy you've ever had or even exactly what a lot of books or experts identify as the best situation for babies. You may also find, as I and so many of my friends did, that you have to or want to use more than one kind of care at a time. On average, American families use two or more different arrangements a year. That's not always a positive, but often it represents the kind of solution I found, that first year out. It's a way to spend as much time with your baby as you can, until she's a year or two old.

For me, all of this worked out fine. And so did the after-school program I found for Rachel when she got a little older.

But there were bumps in the road, as there have been for other families I know. When Rachel was two, we moved from New York City to Jersey City, just the other side of the Hudson River. Jersey City had one attraction and it was the one we needed the most at the time—affordable housing. We wanted a second child and our apartment was too small for four of us. So we moved.

But child care in Jersey City felt like Apocalypse Now to me, especially after the blissful experience I'd had with Basic Trust and Cacilda. I'd foolishly assumed that I'd be able to make similar arrangements just about anywhere, now that I knew the ropes. And many people acted as if it was a miracle that New York had high-quality services for babies. So Jersey City—a real working-class town—would be a snap. I hadn't bothered to do a lot of research. At that point, buying my first house was overwhelming enough. I'd heard from a few friends that if we didn't find anything great in Jersey City, we'd be close to Hoboken, and Hoboken had some great child-care options.

But Hoboken was not really near the house we'd bought, nor was it really on the way to work. So I began to check out the programs in the area, and the first thing I learned (okay, so I was stupid, this I concede) was that Jersey City was not working class in most neighborhoods. It was poor. It was third-world. People were struggling to care for themselves and their kids, and they didn't have much money to shell out for child care. So there wasn't much, aside from the very good programs for families who qualified for state or federal child-care subsidies.

Still, I had to do something, so I began to visit local programs. And it was the first time I came to fully appreciate why all those checklists stress the importance of ratios in child care, the number of adults on hand to the number of kids in a given classroom. In New Jersey, a ratio of two to fifteen—two adults to care for up to fifteen toddlers at a time—was legal under state rules, as opposed to a cap of two adults per ten children in New York City. Even New York's rules seemed to translate into too many toddlers per adult, and happily, my kids never experienced that situation. Basic Trust had extra staff, so no one adult was ever really watching five kids at a time. Often, it was more like one adult for two or three babies, and one adult for maybe four toddlers.

But in New Jersey, one adult could be expected to care for up to eight toddlers at a time, and the group could grow as large as fifteen when another adult was there. Even worse, the second adult assigned to the group of fifteen might be making lunch part of the time, which gave her partner total responsibility for the whole pint-sized crew while she was cooking.

You can imagine the trouble that fifteen two-year-olds can stir up on a moment's notice, and that's what I witnessed on one visit. One caregiver was busy making a hot lunch (the center touted this in its materials for parents), while the toddlers played in a large gymlike space. It didn't take long for a couple of them to contest ownership on a particular toy, and start whacking each other. Not all of them, of course. But small clumps of them. Clumps that consumed the attention of the remaining adult. Given that I was on a tour, I figured I was seeing the best of what the center had to offer. So I passed that center by.

At a family child-care home, I saw a wonderful middle-aged woman manage six kids, aged six months to four years old, in the tiny first-floor apartment of a brownstone building. She was ingenuous and caring, talking to the kids, offering toys and art projects. But I kept noticing the rockery in her yard, and imagining one of the toddlers tripping and falling backward (studies have shown that falls are the most common cause of childhood injuries). And the space in the apartment was not more than twelve feet by twelve feet.

Then there was the program in the church up the block. As at the other center, the group of two-year-olds was huge. Only the toddlers shared a big, open space with other age groups, separated only by small screens. The noise was intense, kind of like being at recess at an elementary school—all day long. I have to say the kids seemed happy, and the caregivers were again far more ingenuous, patient, and caring than I would ever be if I were put in their place.

But these weren't situations where I wanted to leave Rachel. And I was seeing why the actual size of a group mattered just as much as the ratio of adults to children. Kids need to be active and they are noisy. But they also need some shelter from their own storm. Research shows that big groups get chaotic, even when caregivers have lots of good activities planned.

After all this, I decided to use a new center that had just opened back in New York City, one that was right across the street from Rachel's dad's office and could be on my commute as well. Many friends thought we were crazy, but I knew the care was good, and the setting was hard to beat. She spent her days in Battery Park City, at the tip of Manhattan, right along the Hudson River, with parks and gardens nearby. Rachel still has fond memories of the rides she took on the PATH train (a direct rail link between Lower Manhattan and Jersey City) to get to the center and of the kids she got to know back then.

All of this is to say that finding decent child care really can be a struggle, just as you've read and heard. Loads of it is mediocre. Some studies put the figure of marginal care as high as 80 percent. I am glad those studies are being done, and that lots more attention is being paid to improving child care.

Still, I found good situations for my kids, and so did all of my friends. And in the years that have passed since my kids were babies, a lot more time, money, and effort have been expended on improving child care around the country. So there are more choices, better choices, and more help finding good care for your baby.

It is also reassuring to know that despite the screaming headlines and sensational television exposés, children are safer in child care than they are in lots of homes. In fact, kids in child care suffer fewer injuries and accidents than they do at home. Child-care centers have to be child-proof, and playgrounds are usually built to prevent injuries from falls, the source of most common childhood injuries.

It's also true that the Killer Nannies, Baby Snatchers, and Abusive Child-Care Workers are more prominent in our fantasies than in real life.

Less than 1 percent of all the cases of child abuse occur in child-care settings. When I get myself to think about this statistic, it makes a lot of sense to me. People don't randomly hit kids, not most people. Abuse tends to happen when tempers flare, a product of an intimate relationship gone haywire, when people's emotions get so hot that they lose control. This can happen with parents who are overextended, depressed, or using drugs or alcohol. Thus, children are much more likely, sadly, to suffer at the hands of someone they know than of a child-care worker.

Of course, you need and want to be careful about choosing child care. No one wants her child to be in that 1 percent. But you don't have to be as paranoid as the periodic headlines might make you feel. Indeed, what I believe you'll come to discover is what I and my friends have found; namely, that once you look for and find child care, you suddenly gain a window on just how resourceful, dedicated, and generous American women can be when it comes to caring for the nation's children.

And this isn't just paying lip service to children and their caregivers, the kind of stuff that politicians say about how children are our future. What we have here are women who live by that creed. Every day, they get up and take care of testy toddlers, cranky babies, and energetic preschoolers. They change the diapers, sing to them, clean up their spit-up, the strained carrots that land on the floor or in the hair. They teach our kids how to tame their tempers, to share and use words instead of busting each other in the head. They let them use finger paints with abandon, even when it makes a mess. They take our children to the park and push them on the swings. They stop and let them smell the roses.

As you enter this new world, you begin to see, despite the glitches, that women have created this vast, largely informal system to see to it that children are safe and nurtured while their parents work, with very little help from policy-makers or business leaders. Some of that care is even better than your wildest dreams, like the care I stumbled into at Basic Trust.

"The woman in charge of my son's child care was on the board of the local Family and Child Care Association and had a master's degree in music and in education," says my friend Jackie, a convention planner in Florida. She started her son at five and a half months with this woman, who had a partner to help her care for the kids. They never had more than six kids, and it was usually four, with Jackie's son the only baby. "It was the most incredible environment. She took such an interest in the children. She spent so much time with me every day telling me every little thing he did. And he loved going there. He loved the other children. He loved the music. I couldn't have created this environment myself. It was so enriching for him and for us as a family."

The other thing you'll come to appreciate is that the women who care for our children every day get so little support it can make you cry. It's criminal that so many of them earn less than nearly everyone else, even less than minimum wage, even less per hour than the professional dog walkers in my town. And that's after so many of them have bothered to get advanced degrees in early education. With all that, most still lack health insurance and vacation pay and don't even get bathroom breaks. These are problems we need to fix. They go a long way toward explaining why morale is low and turnover so high in many programs. Many of these women simply give up and quit.

It's why the child care we do have is so unstable, and why I can't say to you with any assurance what kind of fantasy you should have of the perfect situation for your baby. There are good situations, born of the dedication of these women, and you'll find one. But it's not easy to tell you exactly where or even how you'll find the right place in your community.

And you will read the stories about parents who are more desperate than, hopefully, you'll ever be, who leave their children in the car or with someone they know they shouldn't trust, because they *simply can't afford anything better*. These situations make headlines, and scare us all with the hideous choices they've been forced to make as parents because we still don't fund or oversee care in this country the way we should. The way they do in France, where 90 percent of all moms, regardless of whether they work or not, put their preschool children in free care. Where infant care is subsidized in state-sponsored creches created just for babies. Or Denmark, where after-school programs are free, creative, and homey, and are considered a critical element of civilized society.

I tell you this, even before you're ready to hear it, because I hope that once you and your baby get settled, you'll join, in some small way, the ranks of people now working to improve the pay and benefits for the women who care for our children. The ones who give so much of themselves to make our lives and the lives of our children better.

For now, given that you are probably at the freak-out, how-can-I-leave-my-baby-with-anyone stage, just know that one of those women is waiting for you. She's experienced and devoted and not ready to give up on the field yet. She's Cacilda crossing Central Park to come to Rachel. Or she's Wilma, waiting at Basic Trust. Or she's Geeta, seeing the chance to care for your baby as a gateway to her new life in America.

You may not find her on the first call or even the fifteenth. But eventually you will.

And if you've been paying attention, you've noticed that I've already been sneaking in some tips about how to know when you've found that right person. Because even when you know you've found her, you may not entirely trust yourself.

You do need to know that the most important thing is her attitude toward your baby. That it helps if she's had some courses in early education and child development. Just as you learn about how to handle your child from all those articles you read, so she learns from those courses.

And it's crucial that she not be trying to watch too many children at once.

One shortcut to knowing that a program meets all these criteria is to find out whether it has been accredited. Child-care centers are accredited by the National Association for the Education of Young Children. Family child-care homes, those women in your neighborhood who have a program going in their home, are accredited by the National Association for Family Child Care. These national groups set standards that are far more demanding than those set by most state licensing agencies. They send folks out to actually observe the programs in action, whereas many states never even bother to look at a program after a license is issued, until someone reports a problem. And fewer still make regular, unannounced visits. That's why accreditation can be far more meaningful than a state or a city license.

So swallow your anxiety, and try to be patient. More patient than you've ever been, more patient than you'd be in looking for someone to staff a position at work. And don't stop looking until you've found someone who feels right.

For most of my friends, the search took dozens of phone calls, lots of legwork, and going down some dead-ends before they came up with a winner. What many do, the first time around especially, is take what my friend Lynn calls "a leap of faith. You don't really feel like you know what you're doing as a parent, and then you're supposed to choose someone else to help out. You're not even clear what they're supposed to be helping out with. That's the part you're still trying to figure out yourself.

"Meanwhile, you start finding out about people and places and looking around and asking questions. And none of it makes any sense until you find the right arrangement."

STARTING THE SEARCH FOR CARE

Feel clueless about how to start your search for child care?

Join the club. Most of us begin in exactly the same place—although you'd never guess that by the time you meet us a year later. By then, we're all opinionated experts.

That's why friends are the very best place to start. Especially those with a one- or two-year-old, since they've recently taken a look at most every caregiver in the neighborhood and heard about other ones from friends.

So start with word-of-mouth. But don't stop there. These days, national organizations have Web sites with checklists, resources, and even local guides to caregivers, centers, and family child-care homes. Here are a few:

- National Association of Child Care Resource and Referral Agencies (www.naccrra.org). NACCRRA is a heaven-sent service, a network of agencies all across the United States that keeps a running list of accredited and licensed caregivers, and can even sort information for you by zip code. Just visit their Web site to get started. This group can also lead you to brochures, checklists, and other information that will be invaluable in your search.
- National Association for the Education of Young Children (www.naeyc.org). The NAEYC is the largest professional association of early educators, and has helped develop guidelines for child care used by most government agencies. Recently, NAEYC has also started a program to accredit child care centers, and it is a meaningful one. To get accredited by NAEYC,

a center must meet standards that are far more demanding than most state licensing requirements. At their Web site you can find checklists on what to look for, as well as a list of accredited child care centers in your area.

- The National Association for Family Child Care (www.nafcc.org) accredits programs run from private homes. This is especially important because so many such programs are run in the underground economy, and it's hard to know if the place has been child-proofed or the person in charge has any training in or knowledge of child development. If you want to use this type of care, and hope to find someone who's meeting professional standards, visit NAFCC's Web site to find an accredited provider near you.

- Child Care Action Campaign (www.childcareaction. org). At the Campaign's Web site you'll find plenty of useful information on how to spot quality child care, as well as reports that detail ways to get your employer to help pay for that care.

- Careguide.com (www.childcare.com) is a very useful Web site with articles, checklists, and resources of all types, and it's all written in plain English, rather than in some sort of jargon intelligible only to those who already have a degree in early education. You'll find help on everything from how to find infant care or backup care when regular arrangements fall through to some tips on how to tame a tantrum in the supermarket. Well, okay, that comes some time after your leave is over. But you'll be glad you read it, all the same.

Chapter 10

Getting Back to Work

T he main thing I remember my first day back at work after I had Daniel is nothing. Not a thing.

Well, that's not exactly true.

What I don't remember is what happened, exactly. What I do remember is how I felt.

I remember really appreciating that I had the kind of job where I didn't have to produce anything in particular that first day. I also remember feeling lucky, for the first time since I'd been through struggles over fertility, that it had taken me so long to conceive my second child. During the long wait for him, I'd worked hard and progressed to a level in my career where I had my own little office. An office with a door. A door I could close. I was also pleased to be at a level where people felt a little embarrassed being rude to me. No one was barking orders or giving me deadlines right away.

That was definitely a good thing, because if they had, I would have found it tough to comply. Try as I might, and as nice as everyone was, I just couldn't hear what my coworkers were saying to me. I'd see their mouths moving and I'd imagine I was listening, but when they stopped, I'd realize I had no idea what they'd just said. It was as if everyone in my office spoke Swahili, and I spoke only Russian and Chinese. I learned to smile, nod, or shake my head, and give a neutral reply like "Sounds good!" or "That's too bad!" depending on the tone in their voices.

That got me through the first day.

When I got home, I wondered how I'd do the second.

Same Place, Different You

I came to see that coming back to work was like crossing some Great Divide, even with a second child. It was if I'd stepped through a mirror, as I imagined I could do as a kid, and found on the other side a world familiar on the surface, yet strangely changed. Or, more accurately, as I came to see, I had changed.

It sounds obvious to me now, but at the time, I hadn't anticipated how deeply disconnected I'd feel that first day. It took all my attention and energy just to focus on where I was. I had no interest in the office gossip. It was amazing to me that I ever had been. I was barely interested in my work, work that I had always loved.

I decided to start with something easy, sorting my mail. This was a task I'd always liked, since it didn't require too much thought and always held surprises. It was one of the fun parts of being an editor at a national magazine. I might find story ideas. Get invited to luncheons, conferences. Sometimes there were letters from readers or personal notes to me. But this day, even this simple exercise felt as difficult as I imagined brain surgery to be, and by someone who'd never attended medical school. I did manage to dump all the obvious junk mail in the trash. Then I moved the rest of the mail to the other side of my desk.

That was my big accomplishment for the day.

By lunch, time was going by both quickly and terribly slowly. What with having to translate everything from Swahili into my native language, I was exhausted by the relatively simple conversations I'd had with about eight coworkers. I felt as though I'd been there forever and could not fathom staying another five hours. Yet I also felt as though I'd barely arrived.

In other words, the first day back I wasn't really back at all. I was still in limbo, somewhere between home and work, neither one place nor the other. I was still in transition.

And my primary goal soon became a simple one, one that I highly recommend to each and every friend returning from maternity leave. Up until you do feel a part of things again, which could take some time, try not to act dumb or disinterested. As a corollary to that, resist the urge to constantly point out how hard you are fighting not to look dumb and disinterested. Don't remind everyone that you are still wearing maternity clothes you loathe, that you have an electric breast pump stored under your desk or in the closet or stashed in the ladies room. Don't confess that you find the office gossip insufferable and the work itself only mildly interesting. If you've never had any interest in your job, you'll probably hate it this day. Don't share that insight, either. Remember, these folks do provide a paycheck.

Most of all, resist the urge to interrupt one of these native Swahili speakers midsentence to ask, "Did you know I now have two kids? Isn't that amazing? And yesterday at this time, I was home with my new baby. *Yesterday*?"

Saying that might relieve some of your own shellshock upon reentry. After all, such comments would acknowledge the enormity of the change you are experiencing, one of the biggest transitions of your adult life. And as any competent therapist can attest, "validating your feelings" is nearly always a good thing. Something that you'll soon learn to do with your child, when she throws her first tantrum.

But sharing feelings is rarely a good idea at work, something you'll instantly recall when you try to do it with the wrong person.

There is one exception to this rule: There's the coworker who has recently returned from her own leave, the one who helped you plan yours last year. A lifetime ago. She'll probably have empathy for you. She'll even be interested in hearing your story about childbirth, your search for child care, and how you're doing now. Then she'll tell you her stories. This will be the beginning of your underground support network on the job. As for everyone else, skip the chat about the baby, your recovery, and how it feels to be back at work.

They just want you back, functioning, doing your job. When they inquire about the baby, don't take them too seriously. Most are just being polite, the same way they are when you ride up the elevator together. God forbid that you tell them how you *really* are some mornings. That the baby threw up, you and your husband had a fight, or you feel like you're coming down with the flu. Or even the happy details of your life, like the fact that the baby sat up and ate his first solid food, and your husband got a promotion.

The point is, no one wants to know *that much*. What they want to know is that you are back, you are back to stay, and you are going to be responsible, even enthusiastic and energetic, in the weeks and months to come.

So don't share your feelings that day. In particular, don't reveal the moments when you feel so stressed that you consider bailing out, switching careers, or winning the lottery so you don't have to work. Your discomfort, inability to focus, and annoyance with having to actually do your job again is likely to be temporary.

Not only that, but there are likely to be many days in the future when you like having a job, not only for the paycheck but also for the balance it brings to your life. The competency you feel from doing it well, the opportunity to be out in the world and have adult conversations and earn a paycheck. Studies show such balance will actually enhance your mental health, because you have a source of satisfaction in addition to your family. It means you don't have all your emotional eggs in one basket. If things get tough at home, you get some relief on the job and vice versa.

Yet the first day back you may not have that perspective at all. In fact, you'll probably lack any perspective at all. That day is entirely unlike any other, especially with your first baby. It's the first experience you have in your new role, as working mother, and you haven't had any practice.

Chances are, in fact, that you'll be rotten at juggling a baby and a job this day. You aren't organized. You have no focus. Not even a desire to focus. There's too much stimulation. Too much foreign tongue. Set yourself a modest goal of just coming out alive, without alienating anyone or acting too dumb.

Also recognize that you will have to pull this off even though you will spend the entire day in two places emotionally—this space at work and that space where your baby is, or where your baby was yesterday, with you. Never mind that common sense as well as everything you know about the laws of physics advises you that you can't be two places at once.

You will be.

You don't stop being a mom when you walk through the office door. You will get better at compartmentalizing things, especially as you grow more confident of the baby's care and get back into your old routines at work. Many days, you may even be delighted to get back to the world of work, a relatively orderly place where people say please and thank-you, and don't mess on the floor. Or in their pants. Many of my friends are convinced that most work is really a vacation, compared with raising children at home.

But on this day it's unlikely you'll feel that way. (Don't feel guilty if you do! I have one friend who couldn't wait to get back to work at six weeks, after a difficult delivery and a maternity leave where she swears her son never stopped crying.) You haven't learned how to compartmentalize your life, and your focus is still on your baby. That's why everyone seems to be speaking Swahili. They inhabit a different world.

So it was on the first day after my maternity leave. I was definitely back at work physically. I could see that. There was my desk, placed right in front of me. And I sat behind it, answered the phone when it rang, just as though I were a real worker-bee. But if anyone had asked where I was, I would have definitely said with Daniel at home. Wondering how he and Geeta were getting along. Thinking about how Dan looked yesterday. Remembering how Dan was when I left in the morning.

Happily, he was smiling and playing with Geeta. Otherwise, this day would have been far more demented, I'm sure. As it was, I was just disoriented. People talked to me and I drifted back to my baby, his crib, his toys, how he looked, asleep on the baby blanket that my sister had made for him. Then my breasts would tingle, and I would know that I'd better pump or I'd soak my blouse. I'd close my office door and pump. That was pleasant, because then I didn't have to worry about not speaking Swahili.

From talking to my friends, I see now that this feeling of being torn between work and the baby is a key part of reentry, a way to acknowledge that maternity leave is over and you are moving on. Just like reentry after a vacation, only more so. For the first few days back, you're still slow and savoring the memories of that other place.

And in this case, I'd be willing to bet that if you try to stop this process, you'll fail. The images of your baby will just bounce right back into your consciousness, the memories of what it was like to give birth, to be home with the baby, all of it.

That's because the experience of having a baby is just too large to shelve or dismiss. It's transforming. You have to digest it, this fact of being a new mom, in all its facets, including how you will be both parent and worker. Sifting through the images of your baby, thinking about what you've just been through, is one way of processing it, of ending your leave, so you can move on. That's why I advise you not to fight it.

Just let the images and feelings flow, and pretend to speak Swahili. It will all go better that way.

It may also help to remind yourself that your sense of dissonance and dislocation is not entirely of your making. Part of your ambivalence and discomfort springs from the way we do maternity leave in this country. Which is to say, poorly.

Statistics show that you're likely to be getting back to work full-time only eight to twelve weeks after giving birth and before you feel really good about returning to work. If you followed the advice in this book, hopefully you won some extra time and a little extra pay. But chances are you wanted more.

And by the time you arrive at the job the first day, you've already put in overtime on the family front. You've risen early, gotten the baby ready, made breakfast (maybe), not had time to eat it, loaded the baby into the car seat, taken the baby out of the car seat, delivered her into someone else's care, loaded yourself back in the car and driven the rest of the way to your job. Emotionally and physically exhausted, you arrive only to find everyone speaking in tongues.

Given that millions of moms now endure this torture, and more women join their ranks every year, you'd think someone in the social policy department—all those politicians and the business leaders who fill their campaign coffers—would have concluded this is an insane way to conduct both our work and family lives. Even worse, it might be characterized as downright mean-spirited that we ask women to climb back into the saddle at work before they can even sit comfortably, at a time when they haven't had a decent night's sleep in weeks and aren't yet ready to leave their babies.

Yet to date, the most consistent vision and advice from policy-makers and business leaders is that new moms should (a) stay home and (b) resist putting their babies into child care before the age of one.

This general lack of support, coupled with such guilt-inducing messages, certainly feeds any ambivalence you may have the first day back.

And then there are the workplaces where people act like you never had a baby.

Or those that give you a day or two, and then convey the message—or even say it right out loud—that you just had more time off than they've had in years (never mind that it was only six weeks, and taking care of a baby wasn't exactly a vacation), so now it's time to *get over it* and *get on with it.*

Which makes the transition all the more confounding. It's hard enough to get back to work after a great vacation. But now you're trying to get back into the game when your uniform still doesn't fit and you have a whole other demanding life at home.

And then there's another fact about that first day, a fact I've avoided dwelling on, but one we all know to be true. You miss that baby. In fact, on this first day, leaving that baby may well have been the defining moment of your day.

The First Good-bye

I hadn't gotten to that part yet, the good-bye-to-the-baby part yet, because I figure by now you might be sick of my telling you how lucky I was about my job and the way I returned.

I'm not going to say that leaving Dan wasn't hard, or that I didn't miss him. But having had the four months at home with him before I went back to work and then returning on a part-time schedule made all the difference. With Rachel, I was utterly convinced that we would both die upon separation. This was why the director of Basic Trust Infant and Toddler Center finally threw me out, even though they have a policy of gradual separations. "It's time for you to go," she said, after several mornings of me hanging on. "You both have to learn that you can do this. That you can separate and do just fine." She was right. We did.

So with Dan, I had that hard-won confidence that babies can thrive, even if Mom isn't on round-the-clock detail. I also had the experience of a week at home with Geeta on duty before I went back to work. So I'd observed firsthand that Geeta was entirely competent and loving and that Dan was relaxed with her.

I highly recommend starting out that way if you can. That is, starting out your child-care arrangement ahead of your first day back, and coming back part-time for at least a few days, if you can swing it. If you're covered by the Family and Medical Leave Act, you can use the time incrementally, with permission from your boss. Translated, you can come back part-time, if your company agrees to it.

But if the statistics are right, it's likely you won't be coming back to work under such circumstances. So I'm not going to pretend that it's going to be easy on the good-bye front. It's usually not. Even if your baby is placid, and most of them are until at least six or eight months, *you* will likely be a wreck. Especially if you're getting back to work only because the alternative is going broke. "I took only four weeks off," says Lucy, a hairdresser. "How could I take more than that? We'd go bankrupt." Ditto for so many other women.

I say all this so you can remember to be gentle with yourself and remember that it does get better. It won't always be like this. You'll get less tired, your baby will be more independent, and chances are, you'll even find some things you like about that job you hate this day. But today, that good-bye will likely be the big event.

And it made my friends sad, made them miserable. Even if maternity leave had been completely miserable for weeks and weeks on end. Now it felt *more* miserable to leave the baby. Some of my friends cried for a few minutes after saying good-bye. Some cried all the way to work. Some cried in the ladies room after they got to work. Some of them dropped their babies off quickly to avoid crying.

Most also describe a phenomenon that I myself felt with my first baby. Leaving the baby that day felt like leaving the baby permanently. I seemed to forget that I would see my child that very afternoon, and every single day for the next eighteen years or so. No sense that a day would ever come when I might *wish* to have a separation from my child. Like when your child graduates from college and is supposed to go off and make a life of his own, but comes home again instead.

At the first good-bye, you may not even have the perspective that you're going to see each other *that night.* "The crazy thing about those early separations is that somehow it feels as if you'll never see that baby again," says my friend Elisabeth. "I got it into my head that if she wasn't with me twenty-four hours a day, all the time, then it was like we weren't together at all. I look back now and that seems crazy. But I remember that's how it felt."

I think almost any mother can understand why it feels that way, even though it's irrational on its face. First of all, babies are helpless. Or at least, you feel that way as a first-time mother. You tell yourself that this little infant can't speak up, except to cry. And as you're thinking this, you forget just how well he sees to his own needs by crying. How well he lets people know when something is wrong. How he gets people to bring him food, toys, blankets, new diapers.

So you're the one who's likely to be the wreck that first day, treating your first good-bye as your last.

Before long, you'll also have the memory of the happy reunions, the playtime in the evenings, the slow Sunday mornings in spring when you can go for walks. You'll see that there are more than good-byes in store. And once your baby bonds with her caregiver, you'll also see why by now there is about fifty years' worth of research showing that babies can thrive when Mom works. Just as you discovered that the nanny is probably not going to climb out the second-floor bathroom window with your son.

It just takes a little time.

So right now, let yourself grieve a little before you move on. Let yourself feel the end of maternity leave, the end of a phase in your lives, those early weeks or months together, time that you'll never have again. It's only natural to grieve the change. "It's so odd to carry that baby around inside of you for nine months, and then she's out, and then you become totally separate," says Isabel. "And then you have to leave her with someone else. This was devastatingly difficult for me. I wasn't ready to go back to work and I felt insecure about others caring for him."

Over time, Isabel gained confidence in both her child care and her job. Like me, she has also come to see that there are benefits for her children in her working.

That's something I often remind myself of. All the things that my children like about the fact that I work. As an exercise in school, Rachel once made a list of all her favorite things about my job. The water cooler ranked number one. In fact, it was a high point of her preschool days, when she had a day off and I didn't and so she came with me to my office. Filling up the little paper cups and drinking so many we had to run to the ladies room at work usually took at least fifteen minutes at a time.

The copier was also high on her list. She learned, at the ripe old age of three, to make copies of her handprint, simply by putting her hand right on the glass of the copier. That could keep her busy for a whole five minutes on a day when I had to work and she was out of school. The electric pencil sharpener was a hit as well.

Okay, so I'm making light of the benefits.

Now that she's a teenager, we have talked about all the things she likes about the fact I work. Sometimes, when she doesn't need me to run too many errands or focus entirely on *her* worries and concerns, she even says I've been a good role model. That I seem to like my work and like being a mom as well.

Which is the truth.

But on the first day back, I didn't have that perspective at all.

On the first day back, even though I'd had a long enough maternity leave, and even though I had terrific child care, I felt lots of ambivalence. I could see that it was not going to be so simple to straddle the worlds of work and home, to inhabit these two places simultaneously, which is what I've done for all the years since.

At first, you're in that place of feeling stupid, like where you were the first few days of maternity leave. That is why I'm going to give you a few last pages of advice on how to soldier on at the job, now that you really are a working mom. The last part of maternity leave is really the first month or two on the job, when you are still riding through this big transition. While you are still stretching to fit into that uniform and learning to speak the same language as everyone else.

The First Week Back

I keep telling you to be kind to yourself. Please do that your first week back on the job, especially if you must get back to work just six to eight weeks after giving birth. Get as much help as you can at home. Spring some cash for a cleaning person, some takeout meals, anything that helps you keep up with things at home. Even if it's a little pricey at first, it will buy you some time and save you some stress.

Here are some more tactics that my friends told me really helped them stay sane during the back-to-work transition:

Get the baby on a sleep schedule the week before you go back.

I say this with some trepidation. Some babies won't cooperate. But a lot of them will follow the simple regimen suggested by the child-care experts Dr. Spock and Dr. Richard Ferber: putting them in their crib at an appointed time and letting them cry it out. If you haven't done this yet, be prepared for the first night to be excruciating. It will be a dry run for how you feel when you say good-bye that first day. But once the schedule is set, you'll all be better rested and happier. If you fail at establishing a really regular schedule, at least make sure the baby is sleeping at night and not all day long. Otherwise, you'll all reach meltdown quickly after your return to work. Schedules and routines, you will see, are the lifeblood of working parents. Without them, life descends quickly to chaos.

Find out what to expect at work.

If you were so confident of yourself that you ignored the advice I gave earlier in this book, and have failed to keep in touch with your office, now is the time to make amends. Call someone up, and find out if there have been any big changes or any in the works in the short term. It's no fun to walk into work and find out there's a big project and everybody's expected to put in mandatory overtime. Or to find out that pink slips were just handed out. Accept the fact that you're going to be shellshocked the first day in any case. No need to make yourself comatose. Find out about the big changes at work before you show up.

Start on a Wednesday or Thursday.

Jumping back in to a full-time schedule for a full week can truly test your sanity. The experience may even convince you to do something drastic, like quit at the end of the first week. Don't do this to yourself. Start midweek, so you can collapse on the weekend. You'll probably find the second week is easier, and with each passing week, everything is less demanding and less tiring. Especially if you set up routines and rituals. Like the sleeping routine I mentioned earlier. Eating helps, too. Especially if you are breastfeeding.

Don't criticize the work done in your absence.

During the first month or so, you may come upon the re-
sults of work done while you were out on leave. Some of it
may be sloppy, misguided, or misinformed. There may even
be some monstrous mistakes. You may want to scream, yell,
stamp your feet, complain.

Don't.

Instead, figure out a way to right the wrongs and be grateful for the work and appreciative of the coworkers who filled
in for you. If your office is like most, those mistakes and
sloppiness probably happened because someone had to do
your work on top of their own and maybe without any direction or support. Preserve your relationships. Remember
you're going to be working with these same people tomorrow.

Allow yourself extra time for everything.

At first, everything takes longer because you don't know
how to do it—how to get ready for work with a baby in
the room, how to get the baby ready when you have to put
on something besides sweats, what to do when the baby
unexpectedly dirties her diaper or throws up. You'll get the
hang of it soon, when it becomes just another routine, and
then you'll wonder why you thought it was so hard the
first day. In the meantime, build in extra time for everything you do. Five extra minutes can prevent a mini-
breakdown in a new mother. I know this from personal
experience.

Get organized.

Which brings up the urgent need for order, even if you've
never been organized in your life. Now is the time to start.
Get your clothes for work ready the night before. Get your

baby's belongings together as well. Change of clothes. Bottles. Snacks. Toys. Pacifier. Everything you'll need in the morning. Establish places to keep life's new essentials, like mittens, hats, gloves, bottles, diaper bag. The fact that you are so organized will be extremely comforting on your first day at work, and for all the days that follow. You'll know just how comforting it is the day that you forget to do it and spend an entire half hour looking for your car keys.

After that, you'll get organized for sure. And you'll understand why all the sane working mothers you know are also the most organized.

The Second Week, the Third Week, and Beyond

Once you've gotten through the initial transition, you're going to understand that everything has to change now. When you shop. When you sleep. What you eat. How you eat. How you keep house. When you do laundry. How you do laundry. How you get in and out of the car. Everything.

Especially the way you work.

Most of all, you're not going to want to waste time at work, because when you do, it's going to mean less time at home. Or more rushing to get home. That's why I keep hearing from so many of my friends that they are *better* workers after children than before. They are more focused, crisp, and above all, efficient. "After three children," says Diane, who does research for a semiconductor firm based in Northern California. "I am exceedingly efficient and can prioritize as well as the president and CFO of our company."

To get that way, most of them learned a few tricks. To save you the time it takes to learn these tricks from experience, here are a few of them:

Avoid all gossip that is dumb and meaningless.

Note that I'm not telling you to stop gossiping altogether, because the office grapevine usually holds a rich motherlode of information about your workplace. You might hear about a job opening, impending layoffs, or the news that your entire department is going to be reorganized—and your job eliminated—before it happens. Which gives you time to be proactive. So you don't get laid off. That's the stuff you want to know.

Taking time for a little chitchat with your coworkers is also just plain friendly, and helps cement relationships. It shows you're a team player and maybe even interested in being a player. Or just getting a raise. That's also good stuff. In the past, you might even have gone out for drinks or coffee with your office buddies. Don't give that up entirely now that you're a mom, or people may think you're dropping out. Keep up your office friendships at lunch and coffee breaks, or whenever else you can spare a few minutes.

But don't waste time, either. Workers in many offices spend a fair amount of time documenting the latest incredibly lame thing the boss's pet did or anticipating what the really stupid office manager is about to do tomorrow. This is not exactly the stuff that affects your future or makes the company stock surge or plunge. It's not even funny to hear about for the four hundredth time. Everyone already knows the boss's pet is incompetent, and yet he's been on the payroll longer than the rest of you. Don't waste another minute listening to accounts of his latest crimes and misdemeanors. It will only jam you up as you try to get out the door at the stroke of five.

Which is now your main goal, every day. At the end of the workday, you start your second shift: picking up the baby, getting home, fixing dinner, giving the baby a bath, playing with the baby, and putting the baby to bed. Hopefully, in that order. (Sometimes, babies insist on doing it differently. Like falling asleep in the car on the way home, which throws off the rest of the evening!)

So starting the week you get back, set some ground rules about your time. "I let everyone know that I can't participate in the gossip of the day," says Sarah. When someone drops by her desk, she isn't rude, but she does politely remind coworkers she has a deadline to meet. When she has a big project to do, she tells everyone *in advance* that it's nothing personal, but she just can't be disturbed that day unless it's a dire emergency. Most days, she gets her work done and is out the door by 5 P.M., no sweat.

Diane actually keeps a "to-do" list on her desk, in plain sight, so everyone can see what's she working on, and can see that she doesn't have a moment to waste. "That little list, so visible on my desk, usually puts them back on track. They don't hang around long."

Work differently.

By now, you've probably heard the slogan "Work smarter," one that was invented by working mothers, as far as I can tell. Most of my friends have learned to figure out what the boss wants and needs, and triage their work accordingly. Usually, that means choosing the projects that boost the bottom line. For example, if you work in sales, you focus on selling rather than turning in a well-researched list of sales *prospects*.

If you work in a company that puts a premium on facetime, your job will be a little harder. "The big issue around my company is just being there, even if you're not really working," says Terri, who works for an aerospace company in

Maryland. "The model employee, the one the boss loves, is a guy who comes in fifteen minutes early every day and stays fifteen minutes late. But what he does is sit here and read the paper," she says.

In that kind of workplace, the main thing that will be noticed when you get back to work is the fact that you leave at five on the dot. No matter that you skip lunch and coffee breaks and get more done every day than most of your coworkers. In that environment, everyone will be noticing that you're out the door at five. Which is why it will pay to follow the next piece of advice.

Blow your own horn.

No matter how great a worker you are, no matter how smart you work, many people will now be convinced that you're suddenly not. Not a great worker. Because now you're a mom, and they believe you're too tired, too distracted, and too uninterested to do a good job. At first, you may secretly agree! But don't let on. Talk about how happy you are to be back, how good it feels to get out of the house!

And then, when you get back in the groove, be sure to document the great job you are doing. You can do it in casual conversation with your coworkers and boss, by mentioning how excited you are to have met a deadline, completed a project, made a big sale. Or you might even do it in writing. "I routinely write a detailed monthly report that translates what I do into what it means to the company in dollars," says Diane. "That sinks in over time."

Don't lose your sense of humor.

Diane began writing these reports because she was hearing some "extremely snide comments" about her new status of working mom. "People acted like I wasn't really working as hard anymore, especially because I did more work at home," she says. A researcher in the computer field, she got even more done at home, without the distractions of the office. She didn't want to give up that flexibility, but she was also tired of the sarcastic comments. So she used humor to deflect them. "At the beginning of a conference call, I just tell everyone that I am in curlers and wearing a housecoat," she says. "They can't make worse jokes than that, so they don't. It really shuts them up."

Go the extra mile.

It also helps to build up some goodwill, be flexible, and see everything as a game of give-and-take. You give a little, and you get a little flexibility. Connie, a manager in a high-tech firm, volunteers to serve on strategic committees, and sometimes takes work home on weekends when there's a need. "I have proved to my management and peers that I am committed and will go the extra mile when necessary," she says. The payoff? "I am now in a position where I do not have to put in hours just to make it look good." And she's able to take an hour here and there to get to the pediatrician for well-baby checkups, or even stay home for a day when her baby is sick.

Don't freak out.

I already told you to keep your sense of humor. That's essential. Now I could say, "Keep your perspective." But you don't have any perspective, since you've never worked and had a child before. Everything is new.

That's why I'm keeping this piece of advice simple and direct.

Don't freak out.

Don't quit the first week back.

CHANGE OF HEART?

So you're back at work, but you're not sure you want to work full-time, or even work at all, now that you have a baby.

Or now you're thinking you'd like to redesign your job to make it more family-friendly.

Here are some Web resources that can help:

WorkOptions.com (www.workoptions.com) bills itself as the "working mothers' resource for negotiating flexible work," and that's a very accurate description. At this Web site, you'll find free advice and links to sites where you can get help in preparing a proposal to change your job, learn ways to convince your boss you should telecommute, and many other helpful resources and tips. For a fee, these folks will even help you write a formal proposal for a more flexible work arrangement.

The Families and Work Institute in New York City (www.familiesandwork.org) is a think tank that focuses on ways to make the workplace more family-friendly. Check out this Web site for research on the ways your company can benefit from giving you more flexibility.

Gil Gordon Associates (www.gilgordon.com) is, no surprise, a firm created by a fellow named Gil Gordon, the nation's leading expert and consultant on telecommuting. Visit this site for everything you need to know to convince your boss to let you work from home from one day a month up to three days every week. Then follow the links from his site to others that offer information and advice on flexible work arrangements.

Hang on to your temper, your tears, your anxiety, and your frustration on the first bad days that happen in the first month back at work. Endure the dressing-down your boss gives you when you're ten minutes late because of a major traffic jam between work and your baby's child-care center. Hang in there on the day when you're so tired you can hardly focus and your boss hands you a really dumb, detail-oriented project. The one his boss passed along to him, because his boss didn't want to do it.

Above all, don't despair the morning your baby wakes with a fever or a rash.

Tell yourself it does get better, even though you're not sure right now. Remind yourself that babies get sick whether you work or not. That your boss often gives you projects that you do like to do. That there's not a traffic jam every day.

This is just a bad day.

That's the thing you can easily forget as a new working mom. So much has been written and said about how stressful our lives are, about how hard it is to do it all, that when you get one of those bad days, you forget there are the good ones as well.

Instead of being rational, you freak out. You have one of those working-mother moments when you think that nothing could be better, *simpler,* than just staying home with your baby. Especially since your best friend or neighbor waxed eloquent only last night about how happy she is since she quit her job.

At these moments, you'll forget that you had bad days at home as well. And that there are usually more bad days when you are in the middle of a big adjustment like coming back to work after maternity leave.

So reserve judgment. Take a deep breath.

If you really need to, you might even try to recall some of your worst moments at home with the baby—just as a reality check. Like, remember that projectile vomiting session in the middle of the night, when you were changing all the baby's clothes and bedding and your own too between 1 and 3 A.M.?

But that awful night did pass. In fact, you'd almost forgotten about it until now. Think about how calm and sweet and healthy that baby is now. Remember that things change. That life is full of change.

When you get to the other side of this change, this switch back to work, you may well decide to make some other big changes. You may indeed want to switch jobs, quit working, or even switch careers. I've done all those things in my career as a working mom.

But not right away.

For now the most magnificent change is that you are a parent. "I had no clue that I would love my baby so much. It's the kind of love that brings one to one's knees, a kind of love that is so transforming," says Robin.

That's what you have to remember on your bad days. That's what it's all about.

Also that there are no neat formulas for being a parent. It gets messy, no matter how perfect we want it to be or imagine it will be. With short maternity leaves and long ones. With gobs of money and practically none.

Women have been doing this for years. Secretaries, waitresses, nurses, cooks, and hairdressers. And now managers, bankers, car mechanics, and executives are doing it too. Working women of all stripes are doing it and doing it just fine.

In the end, that's all you need to know. That is what I learned from my best friend, Jenny, who had her first child six years ahead of me. When I asked her how she could afford to have kids, how she could find time for them and her job, she answered, "Don't think about it. Just do it. Then you'll figure it out."

Somehow, that was the most reassuring advice of all. What she really meant, I think, was just that I could trust myself. I could do it and everything would turn out okay.

Index